URUK

THE FIRST CITY

BibleWorld
Series Editor: Philip R. Davies, University of Sheffield

BibleWorld shares the fruits of modern (and postmodern) biblical scholarship not only among practitioners and students, but also with anyone interested in what academic study of the Bible means in the twenty-first century. It explores our ever-increasing knowledge and understanding of the social world that produced the biblical texts, but also analyses aspects of the Bible's role in the history of our civilization and the many perspectives – not just religious and theological, but also cultural, political and aesthetic – which drive modern biblical scholarship.

Published:
Sodomy: A History of a Christian Biblical Myth
Michael Carden

Yours Faithfully: Virtual Letters from the Bible
Edited by: Philip R. Davies

Israel's History and the History of Israel
Mario Liverani

The Apostle Paul and His Letters
Edwin D. Freed

The Morality of Paul's Converts
Edwin D. Freed

The Origins of the 'Second' Temple:
Persian Imperial Policy and the Rebuilding of Jerusalem
Diana Edelman

Forthcoming
History, Literature and Theology in the Book of Chronicles
Edited by: Ehud Ben Zvi

Symposia: Confrontations in Biblical Studies
Roland Boer

Sectarianism in Early Judaism
Edited by: David J. Chalcraft

Linguistic Dating of Biblical Texts
An Introduction to Approaches and Problems
Ian Young and Robert Rezetko

Vive Memor Mortis
Qoheleth and the Wisdom of his Day
Thomas Bolin

URUK

THE FIRST CITY

Originally published in Italian as
Uruk: La Prima Città

MARIO LIVERANI

**Edited and translated by
Zainab Bahrani and Marc Van De Mieroop**

LONDON   OAKVILLE

Published by

Equinox Publishing Ltd

UK: Unit 6, The Village, 101 Amies St., London SW11 2JW

www.equinoxpub.com

First published in Italian in 1998 by Gius. Laterza & Figli S.p.a., Roma-Bari, entitled *Uruk: La Prima Città*. English edition published by arrangement with Eulama Literary Agency, Roma.

First published in English in 2006 by Equinox Publishing Ltd.

British Library Cataloguing-in-Publication Data
A catalogue record for this book is available from the British Library.

Library of Congress Cataloging-in-Publication Data
Liverani, Mario.
[Uruk. English]
Uruk : the first city / Mario Liverani ; translated by Zainab Bahrani and Marc Van De Mieroop
      p. cm. -- (BibleWorld)
Includes bibliographical references and index.
ISBN 1-84553-191-4 (hb) -- ISBN 1-84553-193-0 (pb)
1. Erech (Extinct city) I. Title. II. Bible world (London, England)
DS70.5.E65L5913 2006
935--dc22
                              2005037991

ISBN-10   1 84553 191 4 (hardback)
ISBN-10   1 84553 193 0 (paperback)

ISBN-13   978 1 84553 191 1 (hardback)
ISBN-13   978 1 84553 193 5 (paperback)

Typeset by CA Typesetting, www.sheffieldtypesetting.com
Printed and bound in Great Britain by Lightning Source UK Ltd., Milton Keynes and Lightning Source Inc., La Vergne, TN

CONTENTS

Translators' Preface   vii

List of Diagrams and Figures   xi

INTRODUCTION   1

Chapter 1

HISTORY OF THE QUESTION   5
   1. The Urban Revolution and the Legacy
      of the Nineteenth Century   5
   2. Theories in Conflict: 'Modernists' and 'Primitivists'   7
   3. Neo-evolutionism and Continuity   8
   4. Complexity and Transition   10
   5. The 'Archaic' Texts from Uruk   12

Chapter 2

SOCIAL TRANSFORMATION OF THE TERRITORY   15
   1. Primitive Accumulation and Technical Innovations   15
   2. Destination of the Surplus   19
   3. Demography and Settlement   25
   4. Social Structure   28

Chapter 3

THE ADMINISTRATION OF A COMPLEX ECONOMY   32
   1. The Cycle of Barley   32
   2. The Cycle of Wool   36
   3. Commerce: Procurement or Profit?   40
   4. Crafts: Centralization or Dispersal?   44
   5. Services: Who Serves Whom?   50

Chapter 4

POLITICS AND CULTURE OF THE EARLY STATE   53
   1. The Scribe and the Administration of the Storage House   53

2. The Sexagesimal World   57
3. The House of God   59
4. Ideological Mobilization   62

Chapter 5
CENTER AND PERIPHERY   67
1. The Regional System   67
2. Primary and Secondary State Formation   70
3. The Problem of Collapse   73

Bibliography   77
Figures   83
Index   95

There are certain moments in world history when a coalescence of factors led to radical changes in all aspects of a society. The innovations involved were so fundamental that they fully altered human interactions with each other and with their physical surroundings, and they were irreversible. Those moments gain even more importance when there was an influence over a geographical area beyond the territory of the society where they first occurred. A recent example of such an event is the industrial revolution, the consequences of which are still with us today. Its effects are visible in every facet of life: economy, technology, society, politics, religion, sciences, the arts, and the way in which we perceive our environment. From its original core in Western Europe it had worldwide repercussions, and the globalization movement today can still be considered a consequence of this nineteenth-century revolution.

Another such turning point in history happened in the fourth millennium BCE in the southern part of today's Iraq (ancient Mesopotamia), where a single site, Uruk, stands out as the primary locus of innovation. Because every aspect of society changed at that time the famous prehistoric archaeologist, V. Gordon Childe (1892–1957) called it the 'urban revolution'. His terminology stresses the origins of cities at the time, but the changes were manifold. We see the appearance of the state, of writing, of bronze manufacture, of monumental art and architecture, and of an integrated economy that tied together the urbanized core and the non-urban periphery. Because of this multiplicity of innovations the period has attracted the attention of many different scholarly disciplines. Anthropologists have focused on the origins of the state, art historians on monumental art, historians on writing, and so on. In the last decade and a half a veritable avalanche of books and articles have appeared on topics relating to this event, which is now often called the Uruk phenomenon (Collins 2000) in order to avoid the evolutionary model that Childe imposed on it. These studies often concentrate on only one aspect of this event.

Many archaeologists devote attention to the interactions between southern Mesopotamia and the periphery. This focus is partly the result of today's political circumstance in the Middle East. Since fieldwork has been virtually impossible in Iraq itself since 1990, many excavators went to work in the area of northern Syria and southern Turkey where the fourth-millennium remains show different levels of interaction with southern Mesopotamia. A model of analysis often used by archaeologists is that of the capitalist 'world system', imagining a redeployment of productive resources into an integrated system of exchange between a core producing high-level manufactured goods and a periphery providing raw materials. This theory gained a great deal of attention with G. Algaze' s book, *The Uruk World System* (1993 and 2005), and has been a frame of reference for several subsequent studies and conferences (e.g., Stein 1999, Rothman 2001, Postgate 2002). But many alternative interpretations of the presence of southern Mesopotamian material culture in the periphery have been proposed (cf. Butterlin 2003). That America is the home of much of this work is perhaps no surprise as it is also the base of the contemporary globalization mantra.

Starting in 1985, German scholars have begun to restudy materials found at the site of Uruk, where 35 campaigns of excavations took place between 1912 and 1989. The restudied materials include the textual remains of the late-fourth millennium published since the 1930s but very poorly understood until recently. A research team at Berlin began to decipher the archaic texts revealing much of their contents in a series of fundamental studies. This research has led to a re-evaluation of the origins of writing. The study of the invention of script had been fully dominated by a long-term evolutionary model that saw eighth-millennium clay tokens as ancestors to cuneiform signs of the third millennium (especially in the work by D. Schmandt-Besserat, most explicitly stated in *Before Writing* [1992]). This idea takes too much away from the radical character of the innovations caused by writing's invention. The inventors had to develop an entire new system of representation that could signify the physical reality on the two-dimensional medium of the clay tablet. They had to create an inventory of signs that was logical and agreed upon by all users of the script. This was not merely a technological change, but one where the perception of the world came to be fully altered. This new approach to the origins of writing is very much inspired by the works of French philosophers, such as Michel Foucault and Jacques Derrida, who addressed the questions of the interplay between physical reality and representation in language. In Near Eastern studies the work of the French scholar Jean-Jacques Glassner (2000 and 2003) has been the most original in this respect.

Other means of representation changed in the fourth millennium as well. In the realm of the visual arts, finely carved monumental sculptures emerged that reveal a high standard of technical skill and a new conception of monumentality, but what is perhaps even more fascinating is that the representational arts began to make use of visual narratives for the first time. These visual images that clearly refer to mytho-historical events or rituals are a new conception of narration by means of image, and were to have a significant impact on the representational arts in general. Writing and visual narrative were both new technologies that had a profound effect on the way that people conceived of the world around them. This issue has been recently addressed in the work of Zainab Bahrani (e.g., 2002). At the same time, monumental architecture at a previously unknown scale and level of technical skill and planning appeared in Uruk, yet it is not simply the technical skill involved that is a remarkable new development. Architecture of massive proportions, and with designs that are clearly pre-planned with the idea of representing power, wealth or magnificence appears here for the first time. The conception of architecture as a representational medium in its own right is thus another innovation of the Uruk revolution.

Several of the multiple Uruk period innovations continued to be investigated in the last decade along lines laid out in earlier scholarship. The origins of the state are still mostly explained within the context of a gradual evolution from the chiefdom under a headman to a less egalitarian state (e.g., Stein and Rothman 1994), using a 1970s model. The concurrent origins of cities are still most cogently interpreted with Robert McCormick Adams' 1966 model of three stages: (1) a specialization of food production; (2) a development of classes with different degrees of access to the means of production, and (3) the growth of a centralized administration located in a city. It has become clearer, however, that the ecological circumstances of southern Mesopotamia played a prominent role in this process. The role of the city as a nexus of exchange in a highly variegated setting of microenvironments needs to be stressed. This part of the world has a great ecological diversity that has always been important in necessitating human interconnectivity (Horden and Purcell 2000).

These numerous strands of investigation need to be brought together to develop an encompassing view of the Uruk phenomenon. That is the purpose of this book by Mario Liverani who as a historian seeks a holistic explanation. This synthesis combines conclusions from previous research in the various disciplines that have dealt with this period with Liverani's own novel insights. For example, he demonstrates that it was the shape of the long fields that came to be used in the agricultural production of southern Babylonia at this time that led to the need for a centralized agency of coordination. He also argues that the administrative conventions and the sexagesimal (base 60) system of accounting shaped the ways in which the people of Uruk viewed reality. What re-emerges in this study is the revolutionary character of the changes that took place. The Uruk phenomenon is not an almost accidental stage in a long development of history, but a conscious change that was challenging to the people involved. The creation of an urban society was a fundamental innovation that has affected the entirety of world history. Rarely did such change occur due solely to indigenous processes and nowhere else did it happen before it took place in southern Mesopotamia. Uruk was thus truly 'the first city'.

BIBLIOGRAPHY:

Adams, Robert McC.
    1966   *The Evolution of Urban Society* (Chicago: Aldine Publication).
Algaze, Guillermo
    1993   *The Uruk World System* (Chicago: The University of Chicago Press; 2nd rev. edn, 2005).
Bahrani, Zainab
    2002   'The Performative Image: Narrative, Representation, and the Uruk Vase', in E. Ehrenberg (ed.), *Studies in Honor of Donald P. Hansen* (Winona Lake: Eisenbrauns), pp. 15-22.
Butterlin, Pascal
    2003   *Les temps proto-urbains de Mésopotamie* (Paris: CNRS Editions).
Collins, Paul
    2000   *The Uruk Phenomenon* (Oxford: Archaeopress).
Glassner, Jean-Jacques
    2000   *Écrire à Sumer* (Paris: Seuil; translated into English as *The Invention of Cuneiform: Writing in Sumer* [Baltimore: The Johns Hopkins University Press, 2003]).
Horden, Peregrine and Nicholas Purcell
    2000   *The Corrupting Sea* (Oxford: Blackwell).
Postgate, J.N. (ed.)
    2002   *Artefacts of Complexity: Tracking the Uruk in the Near East* (Cambridge: British School of Archaeology in Iraq).
Rothman, Mitchell (ed.)
    2001   *Uruk Mesopotamia and its Neighbors* (Santa Fe: SAR Press).
Schmandt-Besserat, Denise
    1992   *Before Writing* (2 vols.; Austin: The University of Texas Press).
Stein, G.J. (ed.)
    1999   *The Uruk Expansion: Northern Perspectives from Hacinebi, Hassek Höyük and Gawra, Paléorient* 25.1: 1-171.
Stein, G.J. and M. Rothman (eds.)
    1994   *Chiefdoms and Early States in the Near East* (Madison: Prehistory Press).

LIST OF DIAGRAMS AND FIGURES

Diagrams

1a, b   20

2.   21

3. Development of the sizes of temples (–) and of houses (–·–·–)
    in Mesopotamia.   23

Figures

1. Chronology of the prehistoric and proto-historic cultures
    of Mesopotamia.   84

2. Mesopotamia in the Uruk Period.   85

3. The geo-morphology of Lower Mesopotamia (after P. Sanlaville,
    Paléorient 15 [1989], Figure 2).   86

4. Uruk: General plan.   87

5. Uruk: The Eanna sacred precinct   88

6. Urbanization in the periphery: (a) The Late Uruk complex of Arslantepe;
    (b) Habuba Kabira: General plan (from M. Frangipane, *La nascita dello
    Stato nel Vicino Oriente* [Rome-Bari, 1996], pp. 239 and 218).   89

7. Agriculture in the Late Uruk period. (a) scheme of the 'long field';
    (b-c) cadastral tablet and its graphic reproduction; (d) the seeder-plow
    in Mesopotamian glyptic (b: after H.J. Nissen *et al.*, *Archaic Book-
    keeping: Early Writing and Techniques of Economic Administration in
    the Ancient Near East* [Chicago, 1993], p. 57; d: from P. Moorey,
    Ancient Mesopotamian Materials and Industries [Oxford, 1994], p. 3
    and J.B. Pritchard, *The Ancient Near East in Pictures* [Princeton, 1954],
    Figure 86).   90

8. Agro-pastoral activity in the Late Uruk period. (a) Threshing sledge on
    a seal from Arslantepe; (b) animal terminology in the Uruk texts; (c)
    tablet with the description of a herd; (d) weaving scene on a seal from
    Susa (a: from M. Frangipane, *La nascita dello Stato*, p. 250, Figure 76a;
    b-c: after M. Green, *Journal of Near Eastern Studies* 39 [1980]; d: from
    P. Amiet, *Glyptique susienne* [Paris, 1972]).   91

9. Pottery of the Late Uruk period (from A. Perkins, *The Comparative Archaeology of Early Mesopotamia* [Chicago, 1949], Figure 12).   92

10. Recording and guarantees (a) *bulla* and tokens; (b) numerical tablet; (c) jar sealing; (d) door sealing (a-b: from A. LeBrun and F. Vallat, *Cahiers de la Délégation Archéologique Française en Iran* 8 [1978]; c-d: drawings by E. Fiandra, in M. Liverani, *L'origine della città* [Rome, 1986]).   93

11. Lexical list of professional names: (a) Tablet of the Uruk III period; (b) Tablet of the Early Dynastic period (from *Materialien zum sumerischen Lexikon*, XII [Rome, 1969]).   94

Uruk, the First Complex Society in the Ancient Near East

Without a doubt, one of the most significant turning points in the course of human history was the transition from a prehistoric society to one that was historic in the fullest sense of the word. This transition was, and still is, referred to in various ways. Those scholars who primarily look at aspects of urban settlement, call it the 'urban revolution'. Those who place emphasis on socio-political aspects, refer to the emergence of the 'early state'. Those who privilege the socio-economic structure (social stratification, labor specialization), speak of 'the origin of complex society'. And finally, those who take the origin of writing as a result that gives meaning to the entire process, and see writing as an unparalleled instrument for providing knowledge of past societies, call it 'the beginning of history' *tout court*. Without underestimating the importance of the ideological and historiographic implications in the choice of a definition, it is nevertheless unmistakable that they all refer to the same process, but in different ways. That process was so pervasive and multifaceted that it changed human society from top to bottom.

In the nineteenth century CE, scholars saw human history as a unilinear evolution, and searched for the original place of the transition between Neolithic 'barbarity' and historical 'civilization' (to use the terminology of the time). The original cradle of civilization – in the theories of the time and based on the knowledge available then – was thought to be somewhere in the Near East; first in Egypt, then, after the first archaeological discoveries were made there, in Mesopotamia. Today, scholars usually think that several centers were involved, and that each case should be studied by itself, without preconceived preferences. They believe now that the 'stages' (I retain the term as a somewhat useful classification rather than a proper historical division) were realized in various parts of the world, with different speeds and chronologies. Moreover, possible influences of one center on another are not considered as important as indigenous developments.

Nevertheless, among the many possible study-cases, that of Uruk – or of the south of Mesopotamia at the end of the fourth millennium BCE – continues to have a privileged position. It is probably the oldest example of all such turning points, and it is perhaps the best-documented case. It is of particular interest to our Western world, which derived relevant aspects of its culture from it – albeit not directly or simply, but through complicated paths.

After the long-lasting Neolithic period in the Near East, spanning from the ninth to the fourth millennia BCE (see Fig. 1), the so-called 'Uruk culture' signaled the first emergence of a complex urban society or a stratified state. In the last of its phases (Late Uruk, c. 3200–3000 BCE) there was a definitive explosion of the evolutionary process. Urban concentrations reached dimensions that were previously unthinkable (as much as 100 hectares in Uruk), and had temple architecture of extraordinary grandeur and technical accomplishment (in particular the sacred Eanna precinct in Uruk). Writing originated, in function of a sophisticated and impersonal administration.

If the documentation on the Late Uruk culture – both archaeological and textual – is sufficiently studied and known, the larger problems related to the process of state formation remain open to debate. To what needs responded the new political and economic organizations? Who were the authors – conscious or not – of the changes that took place? Why was the process so precocious in Lower Mesopotamia? Was it a rapid 'revolution' or a progressive adaptation? To what extent did ecological, technological, demographic, socio-economic, political, and ideological factors each play a role? What caused the success of the Uruk experiment, and what changes were caused by its regional expansion and its persistence?

This volume is dedicated to clarifying the processes that formed the city and the state, within the limits set by the available documentation. Particular attention will be paid to factors of economic development, as they seem to precede social, political and ideological factors, even though they are closely linked to them. I will try to show – as clearly as possible – how the explanation advanced here is different from those current today, and how these views are related to different historiographic positions, besides the differently focused readings of archaeological and textual documentation.

The British archaeologist V. Gordon Childe introduced the term 'revolution' in order to refer to this process. It is also used in this book, repeatedly and voluntarily. It requires some words of explanation. The term is often avoided today, and many scholars prefer to use the more subtle term of 'transition'. To tell the truth, 'revolution', both in the political and historiographic sense, is only a metaphor, and as such it can be interpreted in various ways. In its original use, which is astronomical, it implies a complete overturn of the relative positions of the various elements that constitute a system. The concept of rapid, sudden, and violent change is only implied in certain modern historiographic uses. Obviously, the 'revolutions' that can be found in the history of technology and the modes of production are never very rapid. This is true also for the modern 'industrial revolution', whose concept was the basis for the terms 'Neolithic revolution' and 'urban revolution'. Certainly, the urban revolution did not happen in an instant, it lasted several centuries, but caused a transformation that completely redesigned the organization of the economy, the society, and the state. Moreover, a process of a few centuries, framed by the long millennia that preceded it and followed it, can still be said to be a 'revolution'.

Chapter 1

HISTORY OF THE QUESTION

1. *The Urban Revolution and the Legacy of the Nineteenth Century*

The question of the origins of cities and states has drawn the attention of philosophers, sociologists, historians, and economists, for at least a century and a half. Indeed, ever since the evolution of human history was first reconstructed in terms of universally valid stages, it has been a concern. The most recent generation of scholars – especially those American scholars with an anthropological background – believes to have rediscovered the problem *ex novo*. But more than a century previously, the great historian Jacob Burckhardt considered the question to be long-lasting and senseless. He based this opinion, on the one hand, on the fact that a long list of Enlightenment and evolutionary theories had already been advanced and, on the other hand, on the fact that proper, non-speculative, historical data were not available at his time.

We cannot describe the entire history of the question here, but must start with the 1940s, when the great British archaeologist Vere Gordon Childe developed the concept of the 'urban revolution'. Childe forms a historiographic link between the nineteenth-century theories that inspired him, and the more recent ideas to which he himself gave rise. The latter's advocates often engage themselves with his opinions, although they mostly disagree with him.

The Marxist inspiration of Childe's views on the urban revolution is well known, but it is underestimated, if not misunderstood. On the one hand, it is well known that Childe accepted the general outlines of nineteenth-century evolutionary theory. He coined the terms 'Neolithic revolution', to signal the passage from the savage to the barbaric stage, and 'urban revolution' for the passage from barbarity to civilization. Certain of his works (including one of his latest books, *Social Evolution*) manifestly intended to reformulate the evolutionary models of Morgan and of Marx and Engels in archaeologically documented terms. Childe's insistence on technological factors as the primary cause of progress also gave a materialist tone and an economic character to his explanations of social evolution.

On the other hand, we know that Marx had little knowledge of proto-history or of the history of the ancient Near East, nor did he claim to know them. Marx's attention was focused on the last revolution, the industrial one, which he experienced in his own lifetime. He was interested in investigating its formative processes, its social impact, and the possibility of surpassing it. His detailed and organic model of the 'industrial revolution', much better than his hardly sketched earlier revolutions, furnished Childe with a specific framework of those technological mechanisms and relations of production that generated the much earlier 'urban revolution', obviously taking into account the different historical circumstances.

The key concept is that of 'primitive (primary, or pristine) accumulation of capital', in order to achieve a quantitative and qualitative change in the mode of production that is revolutionary. It is necessary that a given society has the ability first of all to produce and accumulate a substantial surplus, and second, it then decides to utilize this surplus, not for consumption within the family, but for the construction of infrastructures and for the support of specialists and administrators, the very authors of the revolution itself.

In line with this vision, Childe proposed this framework for the urban revolution:

> [Sumer] was still covered with vast swamps, full of towering reeds, interrupted by arid banks of mud and sand, and periodically inundated by floods. Through tortuous channels among the reeds the muddy water flowed sluggishly into the sea. But the waters teemed with fish, the reed brakes were alive with wild fowl, wild pig, and other game, and on every emergent patch of soil grew date palms offering each year a reliable crop of nutritive fruit. [...] If once the flood waters could be controlled and canalized, the swamps drained, and the arid banks watered, it could be made a Garden of Eden. The soil was so fertile that a hundred-fold return was not impossible. [...] Here, then, farmers could easily produce a surplus above their domestic needs. [...]

> The artisans, labourers, and transport workers may have been 'volunteers' inspired by religious enthusiasm. But if they were not paid for their labour, they must at least have been nourished while at work. A surplus of foodstuffs must, therefore, have been available for their support. The fertility of the soil that enabled the farmer to produce far more than he could consume supplied this. But its expenditure on temples suggests what later records confirm, that 'gods' concentrated it and made it available for distribution among their working servants. [...] But the gods, being fictions, must have had real representatives, nominally their specialized servants. [...] Pre-

sumably these had already in the fourth millennium undertaken the not unprofitable task of administering the gods' estates and directing the works on which their surplus wealth was expended.

The picture can be easily schematized and subdivided into two essential moments: the production of a surplus and its removal from consumption within the family. At the basis of all this lies a technological progress, especially in the realm of irrigation, which in a region with an extraordinary agricultural potential, such as southern Mesopotamia, produces enormous food surpluses. These surpluses came to be used for the support of specialists (who by definition are 'non-producers of food'), and for the financing of great infrastructural projects, including hydraulic works and temples. It is the temple that supported this revolution, by providing an ideological cover for the painful extraction of the surpluses from consumption by its producers, and for their destination to communal use.

2. *Theories in Conflict: 'Modernists' and 'Primitivists'*

The necessity of a primitive accumulation of capital, which society could invest in the structural conversion of its mode of production, was not only a Marxist theory. It was a general presupposition at the basis of 'classical' political economy. In fact, at the time when Childe formulated his concept of the urban revolution, the idea of primitive accumulation of capital came also to be used by a scholar with a very different training and competence, the historian Fritz Heichelheim. His monumental work, *An Ancient Economic History*, dedicated a long chapter to the origins of an urban economy in the south of Mesopotamia. That chapter has been totally ignored in later studies of the proto-history of the Near East.

Heichelheim's economic history was fully based on the efficiency and reciprocal relations of three factors: resources, labor, and capital. The last factor took the lion's share in importance. In Heichelheim's opinion, the two factors of resources and labor remained stable through time, while capital was the mainspring of progress. He saw capital in the monetary sense, however, as circulating wealth that could be stored for use in the future. According to him, the greatest revolution lay in the introduction of loans with interest, which allowed capital to be concentrated in the hands of usurers. This explanation, which Heichelheim claimed to support with textual (but later) data, is in fact erroneous, especially when we apply to it the Mesopotamian written documentation of a legal and administrative nature. Those records show clearly that usury, debt, and private capitalism (whether commercial or financial) were secondary developments. None of these had anything to do with the origins of cities and stratified society. Even when usury gained greater prominence, that is, in the second millennium, it generated not social but mostly private utilization.

In essence the very serious limitations of Heichelheim's proposition were a result of his 'modernist' background. He was part of a long sequence of scholars – the majority, during the period between the two world wars – who wanted to study the ancient economy by applying with no adaptation the factors and the laws of the so-called 'classical' economic theory, based on the analysis of the market relations, which developed only after the industrial revolution.

An essential theoretical clarification, needed to surpass modernism, came from the work of Karl Polanyi. In his earliest and fundamental work on the development of the market economy (*The Great Transformation*) he demonstrated that liberal classical theory was based on historically dated and socially motivated assumptions. Subsequently, in his broad presentation of the pre-mercantile economies, he proposed a picture of the ancient Near Eastern economy based on redistribution. He pointed out the central role of what A. Leo Oppenheim would later call the 'great organizations', that is the temple and the royal palace. The market had only a marginal position and became important only later in time. In his contribution to a conference on urbanization in 1960 at the University of Chicago, Polanyi introduced the concept of staple finance, based on the essential goods of consumption, that came to clarify and integrate the mechanisms of distribution. In an economy such as the proto-urban Mesopotamian and for the following two and a half millennia, the capital at the disposal of the temple (or the palace if there was one) was not monetary, but an accumulation of raw materials, above all food. In particular barley, or cereals in general, played a central role. Barley was the fundamental surplus derived from the high agricultural income of southern Mesopotamia, and it was used to pay the rations of laborers employed in public works. The 'finance' (if we can define it that way) of proto-historic redistributive departments was thus the administration of materials like barley, wool, oil, and textiles. The administrative procedure is based on the two distinct phases of accumulation (drain of agricultural surplus) and of redistribution (used to maintain specialists and to finance public works) – not forgetting the conversion of these raw materials into others, especially metals, through administered trade.

3. *Neo-evolutionism and Continuity*

During the 1960s, the clarifications of Polanyi and the crisis of economic history in the modernist tradition could have made possible the acceptance of Childe's paradigm of the urban revolution, at least in its essential traits, and with some flexibility – especially a distinction between individual cases, and a more positive consideration of the secondary processes and marginal developments that Childe had perhaps underestimated.

But in the 1960s the theory of neo-evolutionism also took hold in America. Although it adopted certain fundamental concepts from nineteenth-century evolutionism (in the first place the idea of continuous evolution in stages with universal validity), it introduced important modifications. This brought about important changes in Childe's paradigm, which were not minor. To begin with, the evolutionism of the nineteenth century was essentially based on a eurocentric world-view, on classical historical documentation, simplistic and cursory ethnographic information, and practically non-existent archaeological data. Instead, neo-evolutionism was much more open, pluralist, and based on a vast array of ethnographic and historical data, even if mostly of the modern period.

It is not possible here to give a detailed analysis that explains why there are diverse positions within neo-evolutionism. But two points should be clarified. First, American neo-evolutionism is mostly based on socio-political aspects rather than on technological and economic ones. Second, it gives preference to continuity as opposed to revolutionary breaks. The various cases, both ethnographic and historical, are placed on a scale of growing complexity, according to the scheme 'band – tribe – chiefdom – state' (in the terminology of Elman Service), or the scheme 'egalitarian society – hierarchical society – stratified society – state' (in the terminology of Morton Fried). The passages from one stage to the other are blurred, and above all every stage finds its presupposition in the previous one, being its logic evercoming.

It is thus obvious that the problem of the origin of the state was reformulated in the context of a development from the 'chiefdom', a political organism led by a 'chief' with a social ranking and an accumulation of resources, but without permanent and impersonal administrative structures. The state succeeds the chiefdom but finds its basis in it and takes its direction from it. A world-wide overview such as the one put together by Claessen and Skalnik in 1978 based itself on an impressive multiplicity of case studies that were, however, almost all modern. These examples all could be suspected of being secondary state formations, that is developed under the influence of another case and modeled on it. Visibly lacking were exactly those cases that had created the history of the problem in the course of a century and a half of reflection and research on the question. In this way – as already noted by Norman Yoffee – the origin of the state came to be studied on the basis of cases about which we know positively that they did not give origin to the state! And this is the paradox of continuism, to take for granted that the pre-state chiefdoms had in them at least the blueprint of a proper state. And this is also the paradox in the use of ethnographic cases as if they were proto-historic cases. The data visible today are quantitatively disproportionate in the documentation and obscure the few and difficult proto-historic data. Thus, essentially, the comparativism of neo-evolutionists, in its principles and choice of documentation, puts at risk a historical approach to the problem of the origins of the state and complex society.

4. *Complexity and Transition*

The overcoming of neo-evolutionism, however, is taking us even farther away from an effective and substantive scrutiny of the problem of the origin of the state. Gordon Childe's dream, that the theoretical systematizations of the nineteenth century could be reformulated on the basis of an adequate archaeological documentation, was lost exactly when it could finally be made operative.

The key concept of contemporary research is that of 'complexity'. In the most simplified terms, one has a complex situation when the elements interacting inside a system do not all function in the same way, and their interactions cause a hierarchical inequality because some of them are more successful than others. In the past, the concept of a 'complex society' was used to indicate a state with a clear differentiation of its constitutive elements, both in space (cities and villages), and in their internal structure (specialized labor, social stratification) and with differential access to resources and the decision-making processes. Complex societies were implicitly or explicitly contrasted to simple and egalitarian societies, in which the cells that make up the society are all homologous, and thus their totality does not contain additional values.

But the use of the notion of complexity has become so widespread in the last twenty years, that it no longer has a proper historical value. I say this without irony: no scholar likes the task of studying a simple phenomenon, leaving it to others to undertake the much more challenging study of a complex one. Thus arrived on the scene the concept of the 'complex chiefdom', which would have been the immediate predecessor of the state, and then came the 'complex hunter-gatherers', the immediate predecessors of the Neolithic revolution. Some kind of complexity has always been existent. We could say that in the biblical paradise, with Adam and Eve,

God, and the serpent, there was already a situation that was pretty complex. By acting this way a sense of proportion is lost, as well as the awareness of how much more complex a state society is.

One could make up a discourse on the processes of state formation that is in some ways analogous to a discussion of complexity. The age-old questions relate to the primary factors that set the processes in motion. There were technological explanations (going back to Gordon Childe) that saw in technical processes the primary impetus for a major productivity increase, and consequently a growth in size and structure of the society. There were demographic explanations (especially by Ester Boserup) that saw population growth as preceding and causing technical improvements and adjustments in management. There were explanations that based themselves on conflict (war and conquest), and others that spoke of organic growth. Some assigned an essential role to long-distance trade; others denied it. Obviously, each of these factors could have had its importance. Moreover, searching an 'ideal' process will always conflate historical cases that are diverse. On the other hand, excessive emphasis on multi-factorial explanations (just as an excessive use of the idea of complexity) risks making an understanding of the essential elements impossible. When scholars started visualizing the process by means of flow-charts, it seems that it became their ambition to propose a scheme with ever more boxes and arrows crossing back and forth in between them. The confusion became so great that the reading of the chart – and thus the understanding of the phenomenon – became impossible.

There is no doubt that the premises are correct in both cases (that is, the focus on complexity and the multi-factorial explanations). What fails, however, in research that produces such studies is the ideological point of reference, the courage to make choices, and the model whose elegance lies in simplicity. The refusal to adhere to an ideology has led in this specific case to the rejection of the term revolution itself, as in some circles the term is considered to be subversive and unacceptable. Using the word revolution, even in a metaphorical way, implies that there were fractures, painful choices, conscious strategies, and structural reversals, which break with the past rather than continue to build on it. Using the term 'transition' instead tends to obscure the event in a progressive set of turns, or in a natural (so to speack) change, a change unnoticed by its very authors, and therefore devoid of political implications. It suggests a continuous re-utilization of pre-existing structures, with gradual quanti-tative changes within which the setting of qualitative borders would be arbitrary.

Thus, to judge by research in recent years, the revolution never did take place. Instead there were – and still are – fifty or a hundred, or even a thousand diverse cases of transition, if possible equally distributed in space so that all continents and ethnicities are satisfied, but alas concentrated in time around the present, or the recent past, when European colonialism conquered the entire world, and at the same time studied it.

There is an obvious counter-proposition. We can forget about the chiefdoms of Polynesia and West Africa in the study of the urban revolution in Lower Mesopotamia. Instead we can use the archaeological documentation that is available today, and take into account the textual documentation (especially the administrative documentation) that is contemporaneous with or slightly later than the events of the urban revolution. We can grasp the process in action from inside the Uruk culture and then confront it with the model that Marx initially proposed and Childe later picked up. That is, the primitive accumulation of resources and their withdrawal from consumption for the financing of infrastructure and the support of non-productive groups. As paradoxical as this may seem, such verification has never been seriously attempted.

5. *The 'Archaic' Texts from Uruk*

A secondary reason – but of great importance – for re-examining today the question of the urban revolution derives from the availability of written documentation besides the archaeological sources. In the excavations of levels IV and III in the sacred Eanna precinct at Uruk, administrative documents were discovered. These use an extremely archaic system of writing. The system was at first 'pictographic' (that is, the signs reproduced recognizable objects), but out of it evolved the 'cuneiform' script (that is, with stylized wedge-shaped signs) in a well-documented development. This first writing obviously was a result of the urban revolution, as it was created for the needs of an impersonal and complex administration. We shall discuss the evidence later on. What we have to stress now is that the existence of written documents provides the historian with more explicit and detailed elements for the reconstruction of the economic system and its formative processes than the 'mute' archaeological record, the interpretation of which remains inevitably more uncertain and summary.

The texts in question had earlier been discovered in the excavation campaign of 1931 at Uruk, and they were published in 1936. But the first edition contained only a list of signs next to the copies of the texts, without any attempt at translation of the documents. The state of knowledge at the time did not allow for anything more. In fact, because of this lack of understanding, the archaic texts from Uruk came to be utilized as archaeological data rather than philological ones for about fifty years. Scholars took notice of their existence as an indication of the level of development of the temple administration. But they could not use the data contained in the texts themselves. In effect, for the whole period from 1935 to 1990, no work dealing with the urban revolution or the origins of the state, or with related themes, seems to have been interested in knowing what the archaic texts from Uruk say.

The situation changed only in recent years, thanks to the work of the Berlin project dedicated to a definitive and complete edition of the archaic texts. It re-examined all aspects, from the archaeological context to systems of numbering, from the layout to a classification of the contents. On one side, the clarification of the various systems of numbering employed for different categories of realia, has furnished the key for accessing the accounting mechanisms. On the other side, it was above all the study of the lexical texts (that is, lists of signs or groups of signs, catalogued by subject) with their strong conservatism in form and the possibility to compare earlier with later versions that furnished the key for the reading of many signs.

Besides providing reliable editions of the texts, the Berlin project has also produced a lot of research on the economy and the administration of archaic Uruk. That has an obvious relevance for the study of the productive and redistributive processes that formed the foundation of the urban revolution. The publication in 1990 of the catalogue of an exhibition in Berlin on the archaic texts and the first systems of state administration has put a richness of data of the first order at the disposal of the historian who is not a specialist. From this work – and from other studies that are more narrowly focused – emerges clearly that there was an extraordinary continuity between the archaic and later Sumerian texts, both in their general themes and in specific aspects. This is not only true for the lexical texts, but also for various types of administrative texts. In essence, the criteria and the procedures of the redistributive economy that we know better in the later Early Dynastic IIIB (2500–2350 BCE) and Neo-Sumerian (2100–2000 BCE) periods were already solidly established in the period of Uruk IV-III (the Late Uruk period in the archaeological terminology, that is, 3200–3000 BCE).

In a certain sense, the utilization of texts turned upside down the perspective on the urban revolution that we had gained from the use of archaeological data of the material culture. It is, in fact, obvious that a study on the basis of archaeological material stressed relationships of continuity – albeit with change – with *earlier* periods. A study on the basis of texts, established relations of continuity with *later* periods. Now, it is clear that both documentary classes should be used, and possibly correlated. A correct evaluation must keep account of both retrospective and prospective views. But it is also clear that an emphasis of 'prehistoric' kind tends inevitably to underline the elements of continuity, while an emphasis of 'historical' kind evidences above all the elements of revolution and the beginning of a new era – or at least of a new organization of the economy, society, and the state.

Chapter 2

SOCIAL TRANSFORMATION OF THE TERRITORY

1. *Primitive Accumulation and Technical Innovations*

The question of the primitive accumulation of agricultural surpluses in terms that can be verified archaeologically can be put in the following way. Can we identify technical factors, or factors of another nature, that increased agricultural production at an accelerated rate, that is, higher than the rate of demographic growth, in the phases immediately before the urban and managerial rise of the great city of Uruk (i.e., the Late Uruk period, c. 3200–3000 BCE)? As we will see, the answer comes from a complex of innovations that developed previously during the Early Uruk period (c. 3500–3200 BCE). There is so much correlation between the innovations that they compose an organic and indivisible whole. The relevant documentation is only partly understood, and it has not yet been adequately evaluated. Certainly it has not been put to use with reference to the problem of the urban revolution.

The Long Field
The necessity of a hydraulic management of Lower Mesopotamia, was well known in the time of V. Gordon Childe (see, e.g., the passage cited above). It was an indispensable factor for the growth of population and production, and for the organizations that were characteristic of the earliest urbanization. Nineteenth-century scholars already pointed out the coincidence between the zones of irrigated alluvium and the sites of the earliest civilizations. This insight gave rise to the notorious (and certainly abnormal) theory of 'hydraulic despotism' as developed by Karl Wittfogel.

Only recently has it been made clear how the crucial stage in the process was the establishment of a system of long fields and the use of furrow irrigation (Fig. 7a). In the Lower Mesopotamian alluvium two systems of irrigation are attested historically. They are quite different from each other: one uses basins, the other furrows. They are respectively best adapted to the two hydrological and geo-morphological zones of the 'valley' and the 'delta'.

Basin irrigation consists of a complete submersion of the field under a thin layer of water, which is rapidly absorbed by the terrain through vertical percolation. It was practised in square fields enclosed by low embankments. These fields were necessarily of modest dimensions, and were perfectly horizontal, since otherwise the submersion would not be homogeneous. A single family could arrange a field by itself, and there was little need for coordination between adjacent fields. Therefore, basin irrigation brought about exploitation at the level of the family or of the village. There was a systematization of the watercourses in the region through piecemeal and progressive adjustments, without the need for special planning or centralization.

On the other hand, irrigation by furrows came to be practised in long fields, narrow parallel strips that extended in length for many hundreds of meters. The field had slight and regular slopes, with a 'head' adjacent to the canal from which the water was drawn and a 'bottom' in marshes or drainage basins. The water inundated only the furrows and the terrain was irrigated through horizontal percolation. Given their dimensions and the strict positioning relative to the canals, these fields could be conveniently arranged only in a coordinated and planned manner. An extensive area had to be developed *ex novo*, with great blocks of fields placed in parallel lines following a 'herringbone pattern' off the two sides of the canal. The slope of the terrain was adapted to the morphology of the delta, since the canals inside dikes were raised above the fields, as a result of the buildup of sediment, and there were lateral basins or marshes for the release of excess water. The long fields therefore required the presence of a central coordinating agency for their planning and management. Once installed, they allowed productivity on a large scale, and they were connected to other innovations that we will discuss presently.

Later documentation shows that long fields were the prevalent shape of fields in southern Lower Mesopotamia, but they are already well represented in the archaic administrative documentation from the Uruk III period, from both the south and the north of Lower Mesopotamia. The form of the archaic Sumerian sign for 'field' (gan$_2$) itself implies the shape. The sign clearly represents a block of long fields, laid out perpendicularly to a canal. The archaic administrative texts document that long fields were organized in large blocks and were centrally managed, that is, by the temple.

The Seeder-plow

The cultivation of the long field is closely connected to the introduction of a plow pulled by animals. Only such a plow allowed the digging of straight furrows with a length of many hundreds of meters. The plow itself could have contributed to the layout of the long fields (albeit only secondarily, after the problem of irrigation had been addressed): the length reduced the number of turns and repositionings of the plow since fewer furrows were needed. Later texts document that the plow was pulled by two or three pairs of oxen, and was thus far from easy to manage. Yet, it is evident that using a plow pulled by animals saved an enormous amount of time, when compared to the execution of the same work by hoe, the number of persons employed being equal. The three elements, long field, channel irrigation, and plows with animal traction, were so closely connected and formed such an organic unit, that one cannot imagine the system to function without the presence of one of the three.

At the time of sowing, the plow with animal traction was turned into a seeder-plow (Fig. 7d), by installing a funnel that placed the seeds individually deep inside the furrow. The use of the seeder-plow minimized the loss of seed when compared to their dispersion by hand. It increased the yield by about fifty percent. This helps to explain the very high productivity of cereal-cultivation in Lower Mesopotamia, which Herodotus mentioned and is confirmed by the cuneiform data. The level of productivity recorded would be unbelievable with a system of broadcasting seed. The placement of single seeds deep inside the furrow was feasible only with a seeder-plow pulled by animals. Doing this manually would have required an enormous amount of time and effort. Although complete representations of the seeder-plow appear in later periods only, the Sumerian sign that indicates it, *apin*, is already well attested in the archaic documents of Uruk IV and III.

The Threshing Sledge

The use of animal traction – with its consequent saving of time and labor – also affected two other operations: threshing and the transport of the harvest. Threshing was done on specially prepared threshing floors, using a sledge pulled by an ass. Numerous rows of flint blades were inserted at the bottom of these sledges (Fig. 8a). The Romans called such pieces of equipment *tribulum*, and they were still attested in the modern era in large parts of the Near East and the Mediterranean before the advent of mechanization. There are iconographic representations of such sledges dating to the Uruk period, and there are also concentrations of flint blades that can only be explained as having been part of a threshing sledge. The characteristic polish that flint blades acquire when they are repeatedly used to cut ears of cereal, and that traditionally is attributed to blades in harvesting sickles, can just as well result from their use in the threshing sledge.

Among the archaic signs of Uruk IV and III is also one depicting a four-wheeled wagon, seemingly used for the transport of the harvest, although the sign is rare. In general, the spread of animal traction happened in what is called the 'secondary agricultural revolution', after the first one at the start of the Neolithic. This 'secondary revolution' took place in the millennium before the process of the earliest urbanization. We should note, however, that in Lower Mesopotamia, as well as in the Nile valley and in alluvial valleys in general, the most economical and efficient means of transporting the harvest, from the fields to the threshing floors and from the threshing floors to the storage houses, was by boats. These could use the system of canals and river branches.

Clay Sickles
Finally, the people reaping the great expanses of cereals used clay sickles as tools, crescent shaped and with sharpened internal edges. The manufacturing cost was very low when compared to other types of blades (of flint, not to speak of metal not used at that time), and therefore made possible the simultaneous use of numerous manual laborers. The clay sickle presumably was disposable, since the sharpness of the edge deteriorated rapidly and could not be restored. It is characteristic of Lower Mesopotamia in the Late Ubaid and Early Uruk periods, that is, exactly in the formative period of the system of intensive cereal-cultivation delineated here.

The dating of this complex of innovations is not easy, if we examine them one by one. It is certain that the use of the long field was already established in the Late Uruk period, and it had already spread to the north of Lower Mesopotamia, where it was certainly not the most obvious layout of a field. The same can be said for the seeder-plow and the threshing sledge, which were present in the earliest attestations of writing and iconography. Because of the material from which they were made, the sickles of clay are the only element of the complex that is archaeologically quite visible. They are found throughout the Late Ubaid and Early Uruk periods, to be eventually displaced by another type of tool, differently from the other innovations, which remained in use for millennia later on. If one examines these innovations together, they all occurred close to the great demographic and organizational explosion of the Late Uruk period. They could not have emerged long after the mature Ubaid phase, and they must have been fully established when the organizational structure of Late Uruk reached its height.

We can propose a timing involving two-stages. The clay sickle was introduced quite early in the Ubaid period. This implies an intensification of cereal cultivation, but its use is not necessarily tied to the other innovations. On the other hand, the more important innovations are closely interconnected, and can be placed just before the Uruk period, that is around 3500 BCE. We can also suggest that these innovations were precipitated by nature; around that time the sea level of the Gulf rose and could have determined the conditions in the delta that made the system of long fields most suitable: small gradients, major sedimentation, and a disparity in level between the rivers and canals and the surrounding countryside.

This complex of innovations – based on an organic hydraulic arrangement of the territory and on the use of animal traction – must have had an impact on the agricultural production of Lower Mesopotamia, no less important than the introduction of mechanization in modern agriculture. We can attempt to make some more specific calculations of the impact. It has already been said that the sowing by seeder-plow increased productivity by an estimated fifty percent when compared to broadcast seeding. Also the use of plows instead of hoes had quantifiable savings of time, and so on. On the whole I suggest, not without a certain hesitation, that the passage from a traditional system of family farming (breaking the ground with a hoe, casting seeds, irrigating by inundation) to the technical and organizational structure that I have described here, would have brought about an increased productivity in the order of between five hundred to a thousand per cent – the number of people employed being equal.

We can very well call this a revolution in agricultural technology, taking place in Lower Mesopotamia some centuries before the urban revolution and the formation of early states. It is a historical event of enormous significance, and it is documented archaeologically in several ways. It is amazing, however, how little it is discussed in the current historical and archaeological literature, which is primarily focused on the developments of social hierarchies and administrative elites, often detached from changes in the modes of production.

2. Destination of the Surplus

Let us come to the second point: did the agricultural surplus, realized within the span of a few centuries, supply 'private' consumers in a family setting producing for itself, or was it reserved for 'social' investment, that is, infrastructure, public buildings, and the maintenance of specialists and administrators? An answer in this second direction is obvious, but the modalities of change, be they technical or socio-political, are still open to discussion.

In Gordon Childe's view, the technical factor (that is, the revolution in agricultural technology) initially led to an increase of consumption within the family, and thus brought about demographic growth. Only when a certain threshold was surpassed did a restructuring and centralization of socio-political relations have to take place. Specialists and administrators appeared, and consequently a large part of the surplus was destined for a social consumption. I believe that we should hypothesize instead that, because of its special characteristics (the long field and the systematic arrangement of the landscape), the agricultural revolution was compelled from the start to adopt a form of centralized administration. It had to establish agencies that surpassed the individual family in size. These then came to centralize also specialized crafts and other aspects of the economy that are not necessarily connected to agriculture.

In the theory of gradual transition, which scholars of the neo-evolutionist matrix support today, the process did not transform qualitatively. There were only quantitative changes to the structures of economic transfer within the society, both regarding resources and services. The passage from chiefdom to complex chiefdom, and from that to the early state would have increased the imbalance between the productive base and the administrative elite, always inside a bi-polar relationship. One can render this process as a passage from a scheme of type (a) to a scheme of type (b), as can be seen in Diagrams 1a and 1b.

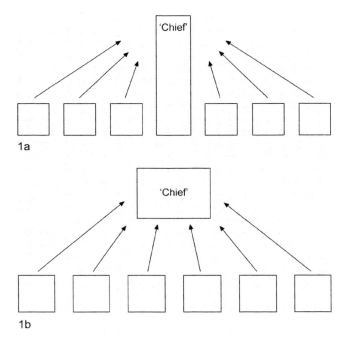

Diagrams 1a and 1b

I believe instead that we must hypothesize a structural transformation of relations, following the introduction of a new element, the central agency. That brought about a tri-polar relation completely different from the preceding one, as can be seen in Diagram 2:

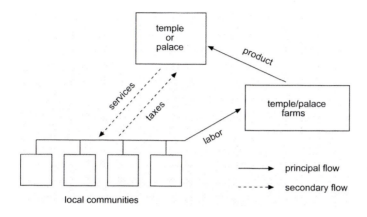

Diagram 2

There is an essential point of difference between the two reconstructions. In the view of gradual development from chiefdom to state, there would have been an increase in the deduction of surplus in the form of *produce* and an administrative regulation of it. That would mean a kind of taxation of the productive unit (family, clan, village, etc.), which is, in fact, not documented in the texts. In the view of radical transformation, proposed here, the extraction of surplus came to be in the form of a deduction of *labor* (corvée), which is exactly what the texts document. We shall explore later on the political and administrative aspects of the process (alongside the ideological ones), which is delineated here from an economic point of view. But it is important to note here that in the new scheme the early state is not a chiefdom that acquired more power, but something entirely different, something innovative and incompatible with a chiefdom.

In a chiefdom the potential surplus derived from technological progress and increased production could be used, on the one hand to increase the consumption within the family, on the other hand to allow the chief forms of conspicuous consumption on which he could base his own prestige and that of his clan. As we will see later, such strategies prevailed in the periphery, outside the Mesopotamian alluvium. In contrast, in the early state the surplus was removed from consumption by its producers, and was destined for social purposes, such as works of agricultural infrastructure and defense, and the maintenance of specialists and administrators, who were not food producers. Moreover, the forms of conspicuous consumption did not have individual characteristics, but communal ones. They were expressed in temples, the images of complex and impersonal societies. They provided the basis for social cohesion and the sublimation of socio-economic disparity to which I will return below.

The strategic choice of the social destination of surplus should have left evidence in the archaeological documentation of the Late Ubaid and Early Uruk periods. Unfortunately, the Early Uruk period is poorly recorded, especially in the key site of Uruk itself, where only one sounding represented it. But in recent years our knowledge of the Ubaid period has become quite extensive and it permits analyses and comprehensive appraisals. It seems that the characteristics of the Ubaid culture, both in the shape of settlements and in the distribution of prestige goods, correspond well to the expected image.

Before anything else, we are dealing with a culture that was quite egalitarian and austere. It lacked a clear social inequality, centralization, hoarding, conspicuous display, and so on. One can think of the pottery, which was mass-produced on a 'slow wheel' and lacked those lively characteristics and decorations that were visible in earlier periods. One can think of the absence of clear differences in the dimensions and layout of the houses that were excavated in sufficient numbers at the sites of Tell es-Sawwan and Tell Abada. The houses are much more remarkable for their similarity than for the presence of gradations in size, to which I will return below. One can think of the homogeneity and the poverty of burials. Every buried person was accompanied only by a pair of vessels of a standard type and by a modest personal ornament. There was no difference in the concentration of wealth that normally provides us with a solid indication for the emergence of an elite. One can think more in general of the extreme rarity, if not total absence, in funerary contexts and houses of materials and objects of prestige and of imported objects, such as metals and semi-precious stones.

The characteristics of austerity and equality of the Ubaid culture may not be astonishing by themselves. But they do become surprising when we see that exactly in this period a tenfold increase of agricultural yield became possible, which led to a substantial surplus, as I have discussed before. The comprehensive increase in the size of the population, as well as the general economic prosperity, as can be observed in the dimensions and the technical aspects of the houses, are not paralleled by a growth of social inequality; or at least this is not shown to us through practices of conspicuous display.

In this setting of a culture, which economically flourished but lacked clear socio-political differentiation, something totally new was indicated by the emergence of temple buildings. Temples are especially well documented in the Eridu sequence, as well as in a sequence at Tepe Gawra in the northern periphery, and by individual examples at Tell 'Uqair, at Susa (the 'terrace'), and at Uruk itself. Out of small and modest cult buildings progressively, but rapidly, developed great temple complexes. They differed substantially from normal houses in size and in architectural and decorative quality, and they acquired a preeminent and central position in the early urban settlements. By assuming economic functions besides cultic ones, these temples appropriated and redefined the old practices of 'communal storage', which were already present in the much earlier Neolithic villages. Storage attained very different dimensions, and very different social and ideological values, however.

We can summarize the growth of the temple institution in a diagram that compares the change in house sizes with that of the size of temple buildings, taking the *longue durée* of Mesopotamian history in account (Diag. 3).

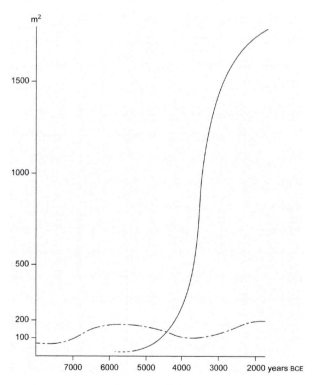

Diagram 3. *Development of the sizes of temples (–)*
and of houses (–·–·–) in Mesopotamia.

The gradual increase in size of temples during the Ubaid and Early Uruk phases – up until the enormous dimensions of the Eanna precinct at the site of Uruk – represents a good parallel to the simultaneous increase in size in agricultural yield. It contrasts sharply to the stability of house sizes, or at times even a decrease in size. The moment of the enormous increase in the size of temples and their absolute predominance, when compared to domestic dwellings, corresponds clearly to the transition from a bi-polar scheme (the chiefdom) to a tri-polar scheme (the early state). It is thus in the temple that we must look for the institutional organism that gave rise to the transformation. Its growth is the critical factor, the true structural change that transformed the settlements of Lower Mesopotamia from egalitarian communities to complex organisms.

For the question of the motivation behind the strategic choices of centralization and complexity that operated in Lower Mesopotamian society, I believe it would be good to distinguish between a technical and an ideological aspect.

We have already seen how from the technical point of view, the characteristics of the new agrarian landscape (blocks of long fields and planned irrigation) directly affected an obliged choice: the creation of centralized agencies. An economic development based on cereal cultivation, that was at the same time both extensive and intensive, required – and thus generated – central coordination from the beginning, for territorial systematization (the relation between fields and canals) and for the use of manpower (corvée). It might seem like a bizarre and reductive idea that the cultivation of barley and the long field essentially may have generated the urban revolution. But, certainly on a global scale, it is evident that other forms of agriculture, based on different plants, did not generate analogous urban revolutions. Other cases we can study show that the surplus went to accumulation within the family, to conspicuous consumption, to competition between clans, to a growth of military overbearing. In sum, these evolved toward chiefdoms rather than states.

On the ideological level, we should consider why the temple was given prominence among various organizations. On this point, I should just repeat to what extent the temple was considered to provide an ideological compensation for the social costs of the urban revolution. Regarding the industrial revolution, Marx wrote that, 'the methods of primitive accumulation are anything but idyllic'. Similar considerations should be made for the accumulation of resources that brought about the urban revolution. The extraction of resources from the producers, and from consumption within the families, and their diversion towards social services, required a strong dose of coercion. Such coercion could be physical, but the use of force is expensive and becomes counterproductive after a while. Therefore, preferably the coercion is ideological. The temple was the only institution that could convince producers to give up substantial parts of their work for the advantage of the community and its administrators, represented by their divine hypostases.

3. *Demography and Settlement*

To judge by the results of excavations and, above all, of regional surveys undertaken in Mesopotamia in the course of the last fifty years, the lengthy Ubaid period is marked by a constant growth of the population. The people lived in settlements that remained villages with standard dimensions of five to ten hectares. The Uruk period is especially indicated by a true explosion of early urban centers, which had unprecedented dimensions: Uruk itself attained a size of seventy hectares in the Early Uruk period and one hundred hectares in the Late Uruk period. This extraordinary phenomenon lies at the basis of the definition of the period as the 'urban revolution' or the 'first urbanization'.

There is no doubt that the growth of cities can be associated with the emergence of politico-religious elites, the increase of social stratification and labor specialization, and the spatial concentration of the activities of those social groups that can generally be labeled as 'non-producers of food'. For obvious logistic reasons the producers of food remained mostly dispersed in the countryside, unless special factors favored their concentration in urban centers. In sum, a bipartite organization of settlements was created: villages and cities. The first were places of primary production, the second centers of transformation and exchange, of administration (in this specific case redistribution) and services. The settlement hierarchy with two or more levels remained a constant factor in the subsequent periods of Mesopotamian history. It should be noted that still in the Ubaid period (not to speak of the preceding phases) only one level of settlement was present, that is the village.

In fact, the urban revolution, with its tri-polar scheme as delineated above, was incomplete because of its very structure: it could not encompass the entire population in a totalizing way. For their own functioning, the central agencies or 'great organizations' (temple and palace) needed the survival of productive family units, which remained for the most part concentrated in villages and provided a supply of manpower. The functioning of the entire system was guaranteed by the relations between the great organizations and the productive family units. The seasonal man-power furnished by the latter allowed the extraction of food surpluses destined for social projects. Even if the emphasis is in general placed on the great organizations, and even if the entire system is characterized as centered on the city-temple, that does not leave out the fact that the majority of the population remained involved in primary productive activities, and remained structured as local communities and family households.

When analyzing the distribution of settlements and the hierarchy of sites in neo-geographical terms, we use to consider the emergence of the early state as archaeologically visible when the settlement structure has three levels: urban centers, intermediate centers (seats of decentralized administrative activity), and small settlements (agricultural or agro-pastoral). A structure with two levels would characterize, on the other hand, a chiefdom that has not established a stable administrative organization. It differentiates only between the largest settlement, the seat of the clan's chief (or of the privileged elite), and the other settlements that are smaller, but similar to the large one in their internal functioning.

In the study of the archaeological record, which would visibly confirm the correspondence between settlement dimensions and their place in the hierarchy, two indicators in particular are considered important: the presence of areas of specialized manufacture (pottery kilns, metal slag, waste from stone working), and the presence of decorative elements (for example, clay cones with painted heads) typical of ceremonial buildings and possibly of administrative ones as well. But it has been noted that these elements also occur in sites of smaller dimensions, so that there is doubt about the simple correspondence between the dimensions and the functions of a settlement.

But in the context of the tri-polar scheme I propose, this lack of correspondence does not present a problem. The early urban characteristics and internal complexity of the major settlements remain clear and certain. It is not surprising that simple villages that provided manpower could have grown to large dimensions. Vice-versa, the decentralized regional administrative and ceremonial functions could be accommodated in small settlements as well. We will see later on, when looking at specialized labor activities, that some of these did not need to take place in urban centers, but were better located in village contexts. In sum, the overall complexity of the system does not necessarily correspond to a diversified placement of specialized activities in the decreasing size of the individual elements that make up the system itself.

Passing from the configuration of the single – 'canton'-sized – cell (the city with its dependent villages) to the larger 'regional' configurations, the situation was not homogeneous. The relations between cities and villages assumed forms and degrees of magnitude that differed from zone to zone, in essence depending on the different ecological settings. In a general way the regional variations corresponded to the already noted geo-morphological differences between the valley and the delta. The extensive surface surveys conducted in Lower Mesopotamia have shown two different lines of development. In the valley zone (the land of Akkad and the Diyala Valley) the development of cities was accompanied by an analogous growth of minor settlements. The urban centers were always integrated in a network of numerous and alive villages, from the Late Uruk period to the Early Dynastic period, and all through the Neo-Sumerian and Old Babylonian periods. On the other hand, in the delta the enormous expansion at first of the city Uruk, and then of other urban centers, led to a remarkable decline of smaller settlements. Within the southern zone there was a difference between the deep south (Uruk, Ur, Eridu, and Umma; there are no surveys of the Lagash area) where urban centralization developed, and the central zone (Nippur) where more evenly sized settlements developed.

Older explanations related this difference to ethnicity or national identity: the south was Sumerian and the north Akkadian. This no longer seems acceptable. On the other hand, the analyses that are strictly based on settlement surveys cannot go beyond the observation of different rates of growth. One can hypothesize that internal migration, from the countryside to the city or from one zone to another, took place. Some scholars have seen the depopulation of the countryside in the south as a response to endemic political and military tensions. But we cannot understand why the same would not apply to the north as well.

If, instead, we take into consideration forms of agrarian exploitation beside settlement sizes, the answer becomes clear. In the north, submersion irrigation of square fields, connected with family exploitation, kept the village fabric alive. In the south, that fabric was partially destroyed by the expansion of canal irrigation, the use of long fields, and the appearance of planned management by the temple. The social strategy of the earliest urbanization was more drastic in the south than in the north, where urban centers remained incorporated into a prevailing family strategy. When spreading to the north, the 'urban revolution' had to adapt itself to the local agrarian and ecological conditions. We will see later that the adaptation was even more marked in upper Mesopotamia, where agriculture was based on rainfall – not to speak of the peripheral mountain zone.

4. *Social Structure*

It should already be evident that the transition from Late Neolithic villages to early-urbanized states brought about profound changes in social fabric and relations. We should examine at least briefly these questions: extended and nuclear families as social alternatives, the emergence of privileged elites and of internal social disparity, and the emergence of a non-tribal social system.

It is difficult to get rid of the legacy of the nineteenth-century grand theories of unilinear evolution when discussing the extended family. These theories saw the nuclear family as the final result of a progression from large and undifferentiated social structures to increasingly more restricted and precise structures. They saw a progression from 'primitive horde' to tribe, to clan, to extended family, and finally to nuclear family. That would have marked the increased liberation of the individual from kinship ties. In reality, the nuclear family is not an alternative to wider family and tribal relations. It could quietly coexist with them. Crucial for us is to determine what was the most significant order of magnitude, both in matrimonial and in productive relations, contexts that are interdependent. The obvious archaeological indicator for that is the size of the dwellings, presupposing that houses reflect the affiliation of those who live together on a daily basis and the organization of labor and administration of resources within them. By the way, both in Sumerian and Akkadian (and in Semitic languages in general) the same term (Sumerian é, Akkadian *bitum*) is used to designate the house as the building where one lives, the productive unit (Greek *oikos*, English household), and also the family unit (at least in Semitic languages).

Primary data and analytical studies are still unsatisfactory, but they suggest that the small dwelling was predominant in the Near East during the long millennia of the Neolithic. It belonged to the nuclear family. Obviously it was incorporated in wider kinship and nieghborhood ties, represented by the village. Larger dwellings started to arise only in the Ubaid period, up to one hundred or one hundred and fifty square meters in size, if not more. These were suitable for housing a family of the extended type under the same roof. When urbanization took place in the Uruk period, the units of habitation became smaller, that is nuclear, and the settlements were fragmented. In attempting an explanation in terms that are drastically simplified, one could think that the extended family arose from the 'secondary agricultural revolution', that is, irrigation agriculture that was administered locally. The subsequent nuclearization could have been brought about by the urban revolution and by irrigation agriculture under a centralized management.

But alongside archaeological information about the size of the dwellings we should also consider textual evidence on the system of inheritance. Obviously, this only appeared after the urban revolution was completed. In principle, the transmission of property from father to son corresponded to the prevalence of the nuclear family. Only occasionally, and in times of need, was property transferred from the head of the family to an outsider. The importance of the extended family is shown by two elements: first, the joint exploitation of family property by brothers, and second, the appearance of more distant relatives when a property is transferred to an outsider.

In the common case when several brothers inherited, the nuclear economy required that the paternal property be divided according to fixed quotas. Usually there was a preferential share for the first-born son, often double that of the others, but this depended on local customs. Joint exploitation was beneficial, since it avoided an excessive fragmentation of the land, which was especially important in connection with irrigation. Texts of the Early Dynastic period demonstrate that, when land was sold, the seller (a single person, or in some cases a couple of brothers jointly) had to take into account a large group of persons. Evidently those belonged to the extended family circle, and guaranteed the legal and social validity of the land transfer to an outsider.

Such textual evidence, that shows the continued existence of the socio-economic importance of extended family ties in the third millennium, derives primarily from the northern zone, that is, Akkad. It clearly fits into the system of village communities and of irrigation on the local level. In the south, on the other hand, the more far-reaching level of urbanization and the spread of centralized irrigation corroded the extended kinship groups, and gave rise to the nuclear productive unit. I will return to this point soon.

Before leaving the topic of extended family relations, two aspects should be noted. First, in the historical period southern Mesopotamian society (like Egyptian society, but in contrast to Chinese society, for example) gave little importance to extended family relations. Connections beyond the nuclear family do not seem to have had greater political and economic relevance than they have in our own modern society. Whenever we encounter definitions of tribal-like groupings in the Mesopotamian texts, these refer to pastoral people, who lived in the peripheral steppe lands and were considered to be foreign. Of course, we should not project a situation backward in time, over one to two millennia, without imagining any change. But the prevalent idea today, namely that the kinship group and extended family played an important role in the formative processes of early urbanization and early state formation, carries the burden of proof. In fact, the urban revolution in southern Mesopotamia seems to have swept away the extended group structures, and to have inserted the nuclear family in larger politico-territorial communities, with possible medium-sized groups of territorial or labor-related nature (essentially created for administrative purposes).

The second aspect to consider is the presumed emergence of administrative elites based on kinship that became the authors of the passage from the 'chiefdom' to the 'early state'. Very much in contrast to certain mountainous zones of the periphery, where chiefdoms were maintained for millennia, such a development was entirely alien to southern Mesopotamia. I have already stated that the typical dwellings of the Ubaid period were characteristically homogeneous in type and size. This can be related to a purely quantitative factor, that is, the size of the family. In extensively excavated residential areas one does not find dwellings that can be identified as belonging to a chief. Building 'A' at Tell Abada is sometimes referred to as such, because it is somewhat bigger than the other buildings at the site. But it is certainly atypical in plan and in function. It is not a large-sized dwelling but an edifice with communal characteristics for ritual (concentration of child burials) and administrative functions (concentration of tokens). French scholars have recently reinterpreted the Eanna area buildings of the Late Uruk period (thus at the end of the process of urbanization) as ceremonial places for the reunions of elders and for communal meals instead of temples. This seems without foundation, however.

We come thus to the impact of the urban revolution on the social structure. What we have already said about the landscape with blocks of long fields, about centralized irrigation, and about the tri-polar scheme for the extraction of labor resources, makes clear that the revolution did not empower a presumed elite, but had the opposite effect. It established a system of impersonal relations and bureaucracy, under the central administration of the temple.

In the entire economic sector that was directly or indirectly controlled by the temple, personal relationships were established between the agency and the workmen. Seasonal labor was remunerated with food rations given to the individual. Permanent labor – that is, by specialists who did not produce food – was remunerated in the form of plots of land, which remained temple property. The usufruct on the part of the recipient was conditional upon the provision of labor; it was therefore personal and temporary.

Possession of land in the public sector was thus conditional and for personal use only. Possession of land in the private sector was based on family inheritance. The two were thus very different from one another. But their coexistence in the framework of the same society brought about influences in both directions. From one side, transmission through inheritance, typical of the private sector, appeared also in the public sector. This could be legitimate, through the customary inheritance of professional positions, which led to the passing on of land concession. But it could also be in the form of long-term use. From the other side, the idea of personal possession by individuals rather than groups or extended families was in time transferred from the public to the private sector. It progressively brought about a situation where the head of the family fully controlled all the property, which originally had been inalienable outside the extended group. He could dispose of it through sales, even if these were sometimes disguised as adoptions.

In complex ways the urban revolution affected the social fabric in two (only seemingly divergent) directions. It instituted large public agencies, administered following impersonal criteria. These agencies acquired control over large sectors of territory and of the economy. At the same time, the urban revolution liberated the remaining (and persistent) private sector from its traditional kinship ties, and started a long and slow historical process toward the management of labor and of the means of production on an individual basis.

Chapter 3

The Administration of a Complex Economy

1. *The Cycle of Barley*

The Sumerians of the third millennium were clear on the fact that their economy was essentially based on two elements: barley and sheep. In a Neo-Sumerian literary composition of the twenty-first century BCE, these two elements boast of their respective merits and their usefulness in dealing with human needs. The text hits it right on the mark. We must clarify then – if only in broad terms – how these two came to be administered in technical, and above all, organizational terms. The production and redistribution of these two fundamental resources constituted the rudimentary framework that carried the entire economic system. Of course, the two elements had quite different characteristics, and did require different organizations of their productive processes.

From the Early Ubaid period on, barley had been chosen as the basic cereal in the diet of Lower Mesopotamia, especially for two of its characteristics: it matures very fast and is very tolerant of saline soils. In comparison to the other cereals that were also cultivated and that had better dietetic values (wheat and emmer), barley had much greater resistance to threats affecting cultivation in Lower Mesopotamia. In the first place, harvests had to be done as early as possible, to avoid the crops being seriously damaged in the last phase of growth. This was due to a bad temporal fit between the annual cycles of cereal growth and river levels. The floods arrived in the late spring when they posed a threat to the crops close to maturation. Moreover, locusts repeatedly damaged the crops. In the second place, the extensive use of irrigation, partly natural but mostly artificial, in the delta where there is minimal gradient and a very high water table, and the almost complete lack of rain, left the salts of the irrigation water on the soil's surface. It accumulated there until it made cultivation impossible. By effectively dealing with the two threats, barley early on became the preferred cereal. It covered about ninety percent of the cultivated area in the south. At the same time, in the rain-fed zone of

Upper Mesopotamia the division of crops was more balanced, with thirty to forty percent taken up by wheat.

When we speak of agricultural surplus in connection with the earliest urbanization, we speak thus essentially of a surplus of barley. The temple was faced with the organizational problem of producing and accumulating large amounts of barley, in excess of what was needed to feed the farmers. The solution to this problem gave the entire economy of Lower Mesopotamia in the early historical periods its characteristic configuration.

In simple terms one could say – and there are indeed those who do so – that the villages of agricultural producers were tributaries to the temple, and conveyed a fixed share of their harvest to the temple. Such a simple tributary relationship is essentially found in chiefdoms. There is no complexity in the system. It is, however, very painful for the producers, and requires two physical displacements of the product: accumulation and redistribution. The selected solution was completely different. The agricultural infrastructure became systematized through irrigation, and the cultivated land became the property of the temple itself. The harvest went directly to the temple, after deducting only the amounts destined for the workers. If all agricultural workers needed in the various seasons and their respective families had been fully supported year-round, there would have been insufficient surplus to be used for social investment. Thus the temple made use of hired corvée labor from the village population during specific moments of agricultural activity, especially during reaping, and without maintenance of the workers' families.

The standard unit of production was an area of one hundred *iku* (c. thirty hectares) of land in the form of a long field. That unit was cultivated by one *engar*, a Sumerian term usually translated as 'farmer', but more appropriately an 'agricultural manager'. He was equipped with an *apin*, 'plow', although more accurately a 'team for plowing and sowing', and two or three pairs of oxen. He had a very small number of dependents that were compensated with plots of land. Seasonal work that required the concentration of hundreds of workers was taken care of through corvée labor. In its entirety the mechanism resembles the 'feudal' system in late medieval Poland as studied by Witold Kula. Actual expenses for running the agricultural process were relatively modest. A substantial surplus could thus be collected. But, if we also take the social costs into account, which were born by the village communities, the balance would be largely negative.

The temple compensated seasonal laborers with personal rations, but unloaded all other costs onto the communities from which they came. Not only when this system was fully developed in the Neo-Sumerian period (twenty-first century BCE), but already in the Late Uruk period, the production costs were calculated at one third of the harvest. Two thirds of the harvest were kept by the central administration. The production costs included the following: seed needed for the following year, food rations for the workers, and fodder for the animals during the months when they were used (for the rest of the year they were pastured in a state of malnutrition). The crucial moment, or mechanism, for the creation of a surplus was thus the recruitment of compulsory seasonal labor. Or, ideologically, we can phrase this in more positive terms: the lands of the god, that is, the temple lands, were farmed by the faithful as a mandatory service (moreover paid with food rations). The 'cost' to the communities from which the labor originated – villages and families – was probably not excessive. It is true that the corvée duty fell exactly when each person also needed to attend to his own fields. But in the context of an extended family the loss of one member out of ten, for two to three months a year, was probably not a very serious problem (if this was the order of magnitude of the labor demanded).

From later texts it is clear that the administration estimated the full agricultural income shortly before the harvest, and then demanded a flat rate of it. This system was used throughout antiquity, as it was difficult to control what happened to the harvest after reaping – certainly after threshing – when it was easy to steal from it. Straw was also utilized, especially for the production of bricks and as fuel.

Let us go back to the productive mechanism in its totality. The tributary relationship of the chiefdom is based on a simple distinction between the chief and tributary producers. The system introduced in Lower Mesopotamia was based on the integration of three elements: the central agency (the temple, later also the royal palace), the village (from which corvée labor was extracted), and the temple's farm. This triple relationship (with further complications that we cannot examine in detail here) brings about a complexity in space, a diversification of the territory and its occupants. Fields and people had different juridical and socio-economic statuses. They also had different relationships with the central agency. Land could be centrally administered, assigned conditionally to individuals, worked directly as family property, or rented for a fee or in a sharecropping arrangement. People could be fully dependent on the central redistributive agency, or belong to communities that were economically 'free', in the sense that they owned their means of production, but were compelled to render service to the central agency. The relations between the different elements were equally complex: there were compulsory labor supplies, supplies of services on the part of specialists, supplies of food rations, the usufruct of the means of production, and so on.

Barley was fundamental to the whole system, not only because it was the major source of nutrition, but also because it was easily stored, preserved, and redistributed. It was the central component of the rations for corvée laborers and full-time dependents – and thus at the center of the financial system in general, in the context of staple finance. Naturally, Mesopotamian people did not survive on barley alone. But the production of other food products did not give rise to analogous cycles of management, essentially for technical reasons. For example, onions or lettuces could not be stored, because they mould or rot rapidly. For that reason all people cultivated their own vegetables and the temple did not interfere. The date palm was of great importance to provide sweeteners, and was part of the agricultural landscape of Lower Mesopotamia from the Ubaid period on. The tree required constant specialized care throughout the year, and was thus unsuited for forced labor, and better suited for families, sharecroppers, and tenants.

I do not believe that there has been enough reflection on the peculiar influence of barley, with its special characteristics, in the process of early urbanization. A comparison with other agricultural situations will clarify this point.

On the one hand, we can consider agriculture based on the cultivation of tubers and fruits, prevalent in tropical and sub-tropical lands. It insures an abundance of food with modest labor requirements for the human community. These tropical products do not need a concentration of labor, neither when the terrain is prepared nor when there is sowing and harvesting. They are not suited for collection in a central place or for redistribution, because they cannot be preserved for long. Therefore the cultivation of yams, taros, or bananas cannot generate a centralized and redistributive system. Instead it maintains egalitarian societies with self-consumption and self-reproduction. It would be unthinkable to base an early state organism on such products.

On the other hand, we can consider those zones whose potential richness resides in raw materials, such as metals, semi-precious stones, or timber. Those are usually mountain areas, and they also appear at the periphery of Mesopotamia. Potentially the income of local resources is very rich, and it can be centrally accumulated. It remains immovable, however, and cannot be redistributed in the form of food. He who controls the resources, the local chief, can enrich himself by integrating himself into exchange systems, but the local population remains cut off from this process, except for a small number of miners or wood-cutters. With the technology of the time, basic food products could not 'be exchanged' because they could not be transported at a reasonable cost. Such an economy can generate processes of treasuring, conspicuous display for prestige purposes, but not processes of urbanization and centralization. This situation is dramatically illustrated by the Greek myth of King Midas and his golden touch. He was exceedingly rich, but unable to feed himself.

Barley is positioned right in the middle, so to speak, between these two extreme situations of wealth that is easy to produce but difficult to redistribute. It can produce a great surplus, but only after the investment of vast amounts of human labor, for the preparation of the land through irrigation and for cultivation. Barley can be easily stored and redistributed, even in small amounts when needed for daily rations. It can be easily kept, as opposed to tubers and fruits, but not indefinitely, as opposed to metals and semi-precious stones. Barley encouraged, thus, both accumulation and re-use in an annual cycle. In essence, barley stimulated interactions very well between connected, yet unequal, elements. And these interactions remained at the basis of complex socio-political organisms. Only rice in South and East Asia, and to some extent maize in Mesoamerica and the Andes, have similar characteristics. In fact, historically these crops gave rise, at different times, to similar processes of early urban and state formation.

2. *The Cycle of Wool*

In addition to food, the temple or palace had to furnish dependents on an annual basis with rations of wool, textiles, or ready-made clothing. The central agencies thus had to supervise the production of wool and textiles in great quantities as well. Furthermore, the production of textiles at a low cost provided the same agencies with a resource that was particularly useful for export in the context of administered trade.

The cycle of wool had a complexity that can be defined as 'sequential'. The various phases of production, that is sheep breeding, shearing, carding and washing, spinning and weaving, involved different interactions with the administration. In broad terms, three differently administered phases can be distinguished.

The first phase was the breeding of the sheep. For obvious technical and ecological reasons, it took place outside the direct control of the administration. The flocks of sheep and goats followed patterns of transhumance; those can be defined as 'horizontal' in the Syro-Arabian steppe, and as 'vertical' in the Zagros Mountains to the north-east of Mesopotamia. Horizontal transhumance used the pastures in the steppe during the winter and spring, when vegetation sprouted following modest winter rains. With the arrival of the summer heat these pastures dried up, so in the dry and hot seasons herdsmen used pastures in the river valleys. These became available because of the prevalence of winter crops, that is barley, and because simple biannual rotation was practised, which left fifty percent of the land fallow. Vertical transhumance used mountain pastures in the summer and autumn, and foothill pastures in the winter and spring. In both cases the breeding of sheep took place outside the reach of the administrators, and at a distance that increased in certain seasons.

The administrative units entrusted the flocks to shepherds, who each supervised a group of between one- or two-hundred sheep, and were scattered throughout the area. The administration was thus unable to observe the real and variable growth of individual flocks, accounting for births and deaths, and their production of wool and dairy products. It could only perform controls annually, or at most every six months, and establish fixed quota of growth and productivity. Those quota were kept low, but could be strictly enforced. Throughout Mesopotamian history, the administration demanded a fixed rate of growth of twenty-five percent per year, or of one newborn for every two female adult sheep. The ratio of newborn male to female sheep was fixed at one to one. Over time, the rate of growth was determined in various ways. The Neo-Sumerian administration demanded one newborn for every two adult females, and ignored deaths in the herd altogether. In later periods more realistic standards were set; higher birth rates were compensated for by death rates, so that the result was still the same. From the archaic texts of the Uruk IV and III periods that deal with annual controls, we can verify that the Neo-Sumerian conventions were already in use with the advent of urbanization. Animals slaughtered for the owner, in this case the temple, and used as sacrifices and at banquets, were deducted from the totals. But these uses were kept at a modest level, below twenty-five percent, so that the size of the flocks tended to remain constant over time.

Thus the contracts conventionally assumed a relatively low growth-rate of the flocks. In reality each sheep gives birth to one lamb a year, so the shepherd was allowed to set aside a group of animals for his own use and profit. This also compensated him for losses in years without growth. The amounts of dairy products that were consigned to the central agency were modest as well. These were butter and cheese, as milk could not be centrally stored with the technology of the time. On the other hand, the amounts of wool that were demanded seem to have been realistic, usually set at two *mina* (almost one kilogram) per sheep, since the administration could effectively control shearing. The temple could thus not collect particular quotas of surplus in the breeding phase, and had to satisfy itself with not losing too much.

Shearing required a high concentration of manpower for a short period of time. So we see here the same system as adopted for the barley harvest. Forced labor was paid for with rations, but the rest of the social costs fell on the communities from which the laborers came. This phase is documented in a satisfactory manner only in later periods, but the organization was the only one possible. Shearing therefore allowed for a certain recovery of surplus, as compared to the cost of labor. The value of this activity is not to be underestimated. In the third millennium, shearing was mostly 'plucking' (Sumerian ur_4, Akkadian *baqāmu*). That was more time-consuming than 'shaving' (Akkadian *gazāzu*) with proper blades, which would become the norm in the second millennium.

The most labor-intensive phases in the work with wool were spinning and weaving. For those activities the organization adopted a different solution, that in the work cycle of barley was only used in the relatively marginal task of milling flour for internal consumption. Recourse was made to slave labor by women and children, who were considered better fit for this domestic activity and were, above all, less costly to the central agency. As the size of food rations corresponded in a very rough way to bodily weight, they were less for women and children than for men. In the case of adult women, rations were only two-thirds of those for men, and for children they were even smaller, about half the amount. This type of slave manpower involving hundreds of people came to be concentrated in special buildings, which were between prisons and textile factories in nature. Guards and overseers could easily control the production. It was not explicitly calculated, but it is evident that the value added when wool was transformed into textiles, was by far greater than the ration payments to the slave weavers. The recruitment of slave manpower came to involve no direct expenditures, since it used prisoners of war and 'oblates' (Sumerian *a.ru.a*) offered to the temple by the community of the faithful. Later, especially starting in the second millennium, the principal source of labor was made up by debt-slaves.

Also in the sector of 'sheep and wool' it is probable that aspects of technological progress immediately before the urban revolution led to the establishment of a system of temple management. The basic technological element was the weaving loom. At this time it was horizontal (the vertical loom was a further innovation of the second millennium), as we can see in the glyptic of the Late Uruk period (Fig. 8d). There is no need to assume that it was already in use long before the first representations of it in the iconography.

Wherever there is adequate archaeo-zoological documentation (as for example at Arslantepe) one notices a very notable growth, a real jump, in the percentage of bones of sheep and goats in relation to those of other animal species (bovids and pigs) when the Late Chalcolithic passes into the Late Uruk. The urban revolution brought about, then, a true explosion in the importance of sheep and goat breeding. This explosion could not have been related to the food needs, as the animals were mostly bred for their wool. Therefore, the increase had to be associated with the emergence of a textile industry, centered in the temple agencies in the ways described above.

The production costs of textiles were much lower in large central factories than in a family setting. This is demonstrated by the fact that textiles made in Mesopotamian urban centers were exported in large quantities to areas where sheep rearing was just as widespread. There are even attestations of the export of textiles in exchange for wool, in the Assyrian trade with Anatolia in the nineteenth century BCE. This demonstrates clearly that the economic advantages depended on 'industrial'-style manufacture, and not on the availability of raw material.

It is also interesting to note that wool was adopted as the fundamental material for textile production in the Late Uruk period, replacing linen, which still dominated in the Ubaid period. That was a result of specific regional circumstances. The contrast to Egypt, which adopted linen as the fundamental textile material instead, is illuminating here. Both linen and wool were present in Egypt and Mesopotamia, but traditionally the Egyptian was typically dressed in linen, the Mesopotamian in wool. This is explained by the fact that the Mesopotamian periphery, with its vast pastures in the steppes and hills, was particularly suited for the large scale breeding of sheep, and favored a strategy of 'extensification'. On the other hand, Egypt was surrounded by arid lands, which favored recourse to an 'intensification' of agricultural exploitation within the Nile Valley.

Another consequence of the Mesopotamian adoption of wool was that sesame cultivation was introduced in the second half of the third millennium BCE. Linen had been used both as a textile fiber, taken from its stalks, and as an oil, pressed from its seeds. A decrease in its use for textiles made it less convenient to cultivate it for oil production. The latter ran the risk of becoming unavailable. Therefore sesame, a plant of South Asian origin that came to Mesopotamia via the Indus Valley, was adopted and acclimatized to the new environment as a summer crop. Seasonally it fitted well with cereal cultivation, which took place in the winter.

To return now to the problem from which we started: the cycle of wool illustrates the emergence of a different type of complexity, not only spatial or territorial, but also sequential. The finished product, in this case the manufactured article of clothing, was the result of a series of operations. Those differed not only in the technical sense, but also in how they related to the central agency and how they were managed by it. This type of complexity was probably new when compared to domestic production, where the entire process – from the sheep to the article of clothing – could be performed in the same unit. It is true that presumably also in the domestic unit work was assigned to different members according to sex and age: children took the sheep to pasture, men sheared, women and girls spun and wove. But the relations between work performance and mode of remuneration were identical. The transfer of this cycle into the central agency brought about the emergence of a range of relations that were completely different to one another. However, they were always particularly well suited as a solution of the various technical and administrative problems.

3. *Commerce: Procurement or Profit?*

The Lower Mesopotamian alluvium notoriously lacks raw materials needed for certain requirements of a complex society (metals, semi-precious stones, wood). These needs led to the development of long distance trade. The trade circulated various goods in the context of an ecologically diverse regional system in which different goods were produced. Long distance trade is already documented in prehistoric times, and can be studied archaeologically through materials whose places of origin can be identified with some certainty, such as seashells, metals, semi-precious stones, and especially obsidian.

With the emergence of metallurgy, monumental architecture and luxury craftsmanship, the procurement of raw materials became more extensive and gained more importance. Within the complex society of the early state, trade was administered by specialists ('merchants'). The relations between them and the central administration constituted an additional, and far from secondary, element in the economic and administrative complexity.

A debate has arisen on the nature of this relationship, which deserves a short mention here. From one side, it is argued that the factors that

stimulated Mesopotamian trade were directly related to the need to procure raw materials. On the other side, it is maintained that trade was
stimulated by the search for profit on the part of the merchants. Both
alternatives are connected to opposing visions or theories regarding the
structure of early historic trade. The first is the famous thesis of Karl
Polanyi that maintains that there was 'administered trade', that is, commerce undertaken by a large central agency, without market places and
market mechanisms. The merchants were functionaries of the temple or
the palace, and prices were set by convention and remained stable over
time. The other view belongs to the liberal classical tradition of economic
history, and has become popular again in the last few decades as a reaction
to the Polanyi's theory. It states that trade was essentially based on market
mechanisms, that there were market places, that merchants were 'free
entrepreneurs', and that prices were determined by the forces of supply
and demand.

One should note that the ancient sources used to support these two
theories are typologically different. Without a doubt the celebratory texts
with ideological value state that trade was administered and that foreign
goods were procured by the central administration. Ancient ideology in
general, and that of Mesopotamia in particular, made imports something
to boast about on the part of the central state. The state was able to make
what it needed flow in from all the parts of the world. The rhetoric passes
over exports, the payments that are required in order to obtain these
goods. This 'propaganda of imports', characteristic of a redistributive
ideology, can be clearly placed in a specific historical context. It is in
opposition to the 'propaganda of exports', characteristic of our own
market system.

In contrast to the celebratory sources are the truly commercial ones,
related to the administration of trade as seen from the inside. They are
preserved in the archives of merchants, and doubtless reveal a mental
attitude and an economic mode that is attentive to profit and price variations. The different types of texts clearly refer back to two superimposed
and coexistent levels of interpretation regarding the economic reality.
They also refer to two different segments of a commercial circuit with a
complex nature. A first segment of administered trade hinging on the
central institution integrated itself organically with a second segment of
free commerce hinging on the merchant. So the current debate can probably be dismissed as based on two views that are both partial.

There is no doubt that the central agencies truly needed to procure the
materials that were not available in the territory under their control. They

could only do so through the conversion of the surplus of their internal products. They had to make use of specialists to accomplish this conversion, that is merchants, who went into distant lands and thus necessarily escaped from the control of the central agency. This is the same problem that we have already discussed with respect to shepherds. The solution used was in fact analogous. For shepherds the administration established fixed rates for the growth of flocks and for dairy production. In the same way, for merchants the administration established conventional relative values (the so-called administered prices) between entering and exiting merchandises. Just like the shepherd, the merchant could thus 'disappear', and return six months or a year later. He would hand over the merchandise he had obtained, and whose conventional value had to be equivalent to that of the merchandise he had received when he left.

The texts clearly hint at the two segments of the trade: there was an administered segment that dealt with the relations between the administration and the merchants, and a free segment that related to the external activity of merchants. Annual accounting constituted the point we can call the interface. Entering and exiting values were compared and verified, and if a deficit was calculated it needed to be subtracted from the next account. Unfortunately, we do not have accounts of this type for the Late Uruk period, but the mechanism cannot have been very different from what is well attested in accounts of the Neo-Sumerian period. These accounts typically show an operation like this: textiles were exported in exchange for copper, sometimes along with other minor types of merchandise (perfumes, oils, spices, and so on), which constitute a sort of 'basic noise' with little economic importance.

In this mechanism, the administered segment was obviously very rigid. The administration was not in a position to know the rates of conversion used for specific goods in distant lands. At best, it could get some idea from the (parallel or inverse) appearance of foreign merchants. Therefore it gave fixed values to goods, values that presumably were low. These rates did not guarantee them a certain profit (or at least, not a substantial profit), but an easy conversion of goods which guaranteed that its needs of procurement were met. We should also consider that on the level of mental representation, prices were conceptualized as fixed and innate to the natural and immutable value of merchandise. Only in the case of goods that had an annual cycle of production, such as cereals, were prices subject to seasonal fluctuations, that depended on the distance in time from the harvest.

Completely different was the behavior of the merchant once he had left with his consignment of goods (for example, textiles) received from the central administration. Obviously he sought to gain the maximum profit from his availability of goods, and to gain as much personal income as possible above and beyond what was officially accounted for. This profit was possible because of spatial and temporal factors. By spatial factors, I mean the different rates of conversion applied in the city from which the merchandise originated and in the land where it arrived: that is the basis of every commercial profit. By temporal factors, I mean the availability of disposable wealth during the several months between the statements of accounting. That wealth could be employed for various commercial operations with their income, or for financial operations, such as loans at interest to individuals in need. Naturally, the merchant also had his working costs for transport, transit taxes, and so on, and he faced risks, such as shipwrecks, bandits, for example. But his personal profit usually seems to have been very high, throughout the history of Mesopotamian trade. It is plausible furthermore that another source of private profit derived from joining, in the same commercial caravan, both the consignments received from the administration, and merchandise belonging to the merchants themselves or entrusted to them by private people. On the whole, the administrative mechanism and the search for profit could coexist esasily in the structure of the same commercial system.

The commerce of the Lower Mesopotamian cities expanded in two main directions. There was maritime trade in the Persian Gulf, where Mesopotamian presence is already well attested in the Ubaid period, as far as the island of Dilmun (present-day Bahrain). There, the Lower Mesopotamian trade routes intersected with those from Oman (from which came copper), southern Iran (from which came stones and stone objects), and from the Indus Valley (from which came exotic woods and precious metals). And there was overland trade that went upstream along the Tigris and Euphrates rivers to the Anatolian highlands, which were rich in woods and silver. As we will see later, in the Late Uruk period overland trade led to the installation of 'colonies' on the middle and upper courses of the rivers and in the Upper Mesopotamian plains. Those reduced the time merchants needed to spend in foreign lands.

Trade was carried out by means of caravans made up of asses and mules, and sufficiently large to confront dangers. The standard load of an animal is well attested in commercial documents of the Old Assyrian period (nineteenth century BCE) at about ninety kilograms of metal or about seventy kilograms of cloth. It could not have been very different in the Late Uruk period. The caravans traveled about twenty-five kilometers a day. Exports consisted primarily of textiles, imports of metals. For logistical reasons the transport of cereals over long distances was excluded, except by boats on rivers. The image represented in the Sumerian myth entitled 'Enmerkar and the Lord of Aratta', where barley was exported from Uruk in exchange for Iranian lapis lazuli, clearly is entirely ideological. It fits into an imaginary scheme, attested also elsewhere in Near Eastern antiquity, where the only export to brag about was food, as it served to 'give life' to foreign countries. In this scheme, the country at the core was rich in people and food products; it was dynamic and self-sufficient. But the mountain lands of the periphery were specialized, with individual products that could not support life. There was the cedar mountain, the cypress mountain, the lapis-lazuli mountain, and so on. Those products became only functional when they were conveyed to the multifaceted land at the center.

Up to this point we have discussed long distance trade, but there existed also local exchange. It enriched those parts of the private economy that subsisted on the margins of the central administration. Local exchange involved the existence of points of sale, if not of actual urban markets (of the type of the *suq* or bazaar in the Islamic period) that are not documented in ancient times. The exchanges that took place in these points of sale were mostly of agricultural products (fruit and vegetables) and of craft goods (such as pottery). They satisfied equally vital needs at the family level, but had less importance in the complex system. They are, unfortunately, poorly documented in administrative texts, exactly because they belonged to the family sphere.

4. Crafts: Centralization or Dispersal?

The specialization of crafts has always been considered an element that qualifies, if not directly generates, the emergence of a socio-economic organization of the complex type. In the classical scheme of Gordon Childe, it was due to the central collection of agricultural surplus that a community could use to maintain specialists who were not producers of food. In the 'Neolithic village' every family nucleus by itself produced the domestic and working tools it needed. In the 'city' a social division of labor came about, with the consequent exchange of food for specialized products. Also in recent analyses of an anthropological nature the identification of areas of specialized labor furnishes concrete proof of a complex society. This evidence is all the more precious since it is the only type that is directly legible in the archaeological record.

Both of these approaches undoubtedly have their validity. Nevertheless, I believe that the importance of specialized labor should in some measure be reduced. Forms of specialized labor were present well before the urban revolution. The new organization had to adapt the role of specialized crafts, more than that it received a primary impulse from their appearance. Certainly there occurred a quantitative growth and a typological expansion of social needs, closely connected to the emergence of the temple. Moreover, there was a more manageable procurement of exotic raw materials. But the factors that greatly contributed to the new order of craft production were of an organizational type.

An analytical category already present in the scheme of Gordon Childe distinguishes the full-time craftsman from the one who worked only part-time. The first had to be supported by the agricultural surplus of the community, while the second could perform his craftwork at the odd moments of time when he was not busy with agricultural or pastoral activities. Therefore only the full-time craftsman generated a central agency in order to mediate between food producers and those engaged in manufacture and services. This model seems too rigid today, too simplistic in its suggestion that there were two distinct stages: one where there was simple exchange (barter) between homologous productive units, the other with centralized redistribution between groups who were economically complementary.

In reality, the organization of labor and the relations of internal exchange differed depending on the specific craft sector involved. Before going further into these differences, one can say hypothetically that a mixed system was possible here as well. The urban revolution was not total, and self-sufficient groups remained in existence alongside the great central agencies. The centralization of labor and raw materials can be useful in certain sectors, but not in others. There can also be duplication, with the same type of work performed in the context of families and in that of temples or palaces.

We should leave aside the recruitment of great numbers of unspecialized manpower, for the digging of canals, temple construction, harvesting, sheep shearing, and so on. The central agency dealt with those through the corvée system. There were only a few cases where specialized work required a concentration of labor. The one case already discussed, that of textile production, remains mostly isolated. An analogous case is that of milling cereals into flour. That was usually done by women through the painful manual use of millstones and stone pestles, which were generally made of basalt. Throughout the economic history of Mesopotamia, the only numerically consistent groups of women employed under slave conditions by the central organizations were weavers and millers. Smaller groups of men were used to draw water and collect firewood, in support of labor teams that operated far from the physical seat of the central agency. In all of these cases we are dealing with labor or services of a domestic type, traditionally performed within the single-family unit. When transferred into the sphere of the great organizations these areas of activity created new organizational problems. In all these cases the basic solution was one of duplication: the operations continued to be undertaken within the family structure, but were also developed in the institutional domain. In each house there was a loom, or there could have been one. Archaeologically a loom is visible through a concentration of loom-weights. Of course, there was also an area for milling flour. Archaeologically such an area is visible through the presence of millstones and pestles. Similarly, the temples and palaces had their weaving factories (well attested in the written documents, but not archaeologically known), and had rooms with dozens of grindstones, for large scale grinding operations (attested, for example, at Ebla in the Middle Bronze Age palace).

Real craftsmanship, on the other hand, was needed for work with metals, stone, wood, leather, and vegetal fibers, in order to make weapons, tools, personal ornaments, furniture, and other things. These crafts did not require a great concentration of manpower. It was enough to have a few people to smelt metals, while only one person was needed to carve seals or to make a piece of furniture. What was important was the availability of materials and of personal skills. Both these elements already existed in a pre-urban setting. The new centralized system led to much greater needs to be fulfilled, as well as a higher productivity and superior technology. Manual skills and technological knowledge were transmitted through apprenticeship, usually from father to son. The central agency thus only needed to bring the pre-existing craft traditions under its own control.

There were essentially two motives for the centralization of crafts. Administered trade brought a regular influx of raw materials, including from distant lands, and public commissions were prevalent, or even exclusive in the case of certain high value craftwork. The emergence of central agencies thus brought about a certain degree of centralization of craft activities. The administration provided craftsmen with the raw materials, and requested the production of certain goods. It paid the artisans as internal, full-time dependants of the administration itself, that is with permanent rations or with assignment of plots of land.

In contrast to the domestic services that existed both in the families and the public spheres, administered craftsmanship swept away – or at least notably reduced – domestic craft production, because of its superior convenience and efficiency. Thus family needs were satisfied mostly by a 'mixed' system rather than a 'duplicate' system. The artisans who depended on the central agency could work for private commissions on the side, after they had satisfied the institution's needs. They continued to use then the local barter circuits, which had already existed before the emergence of the city.

When we speak of the centralization of crafts, we refer to administrative aspects. A logistic centralization should not be taken for granted, and was not practicable for the most part. Certain types of work, such as those that required combustibles, were better done in de-centralized locations. Also local traditions could contribute to keeping alive certain types of craftwork in specific villages. For these reasons it is not legitimate to confuse the rate of craft specialization in a single village with that of the entire territory of an archaic state. Craft workshops which were administered by a central agency can be found and are archaeologically documented in villages, that cannot be legitimately called cities on that basis. Naturally, certain types of production were tied to the availability of materials and therefore they tended to be dispersed in a territory. Others were mostly related to the proximity of customers and thus tended to be located in the city. The extreme case of logistical centralization is found with work on prestige materials, such as gold, that required not only the presence of exclusive public customers, but also close and constant supervision.

We come now to describe the various crafts. The single most wide-spread sector of manufacture was doubtless the production of pottery. These included vessels, from very large jars for cereals to small ones for oils, beer, and other liquids, tableware, such as pitchers, beakers, cups, bowls and plates, and kitchenwares, such as cooking pots. Also small figurines and various other objects were made of clay. This was the most widespread sector of manufacture not only because of the vast amounts daily needed, but also because the fragility of the product required constant replacement. The ceramic sector was also the least centralized of all, and for obvious reasons. First and foremost, its basic raw material, clay, was easily available: it was not imported and not costly. The same was true for the temper mixed with the clay, either vegetable (straw) or mineral (sand), and for the paints used for decoration. (In any case painted decoration declined rapidly during the Uruk period.) In the second place, the manufacture of vessels only required simple equipment, the potter's wheel, which was also available on the domestic level. The firing only required space and fuel. In the third place – and this seems to me the point that has received too little attention – private demand was greater than public demand.

The emergence of central agencies generated a new demand for ceramic products, and used them at an unprecedented rate to deal with problems of storage and redistribution. Concerning the storage of food, one needs only think of the large storage jars, which were placed in rows of dozens of vessels in central storerooms. In the area of redistribution, one can think of a real quantitative explosion in the manufacture of bowls used to distribute rations. The bowls used characterize the Uruk period. The advent of mass production came when the potters of the Uruk period adopted the fast wheel, while in the Ubaid period they used only a slow wheel, that is, a turning platform. For the ration bowls, which were coarsely made and disposable, they adopted a technique of manufacture that was even more rapid, namely making them in a mould.

Notwithstanding this quantitative explosion in public demand, one must keep in mind that the family demand remained dominant. We have only to consider that the numerical relation between 'free' population and institutional dependents was something in the realm of three to one. However, the production for private commission benefited from the new type of manufacture on a massive scale, as it brought about significant savings. It deprived ceramic production of the local and even family varieties that had characterized Neolithic production.

Potters who were included in the central agency were compensated as full-time dependents. The administration commissioned a certain number of vessels, calculating the labor time needed on the basis of type and size. It is probable that the potter had sufficient additional time to produce for the market, or better, for local exchange as well. But it is also possible that, next to a 'mixed' system, there was a 'duplicate' system, with at least in certain villages the survival of potters who exclusively produced at a family level and for local exchange. Written documentation is rare on this point, apart from a few Neo-Sumerian documents that are very explicit in the calculation of the labor time needed for various types of vessels. This lack of documentation should not surprise us, when we keep in mind that the organization of this type of craft was so open and decentralized.

Metallurgy was a very different case. It was already practiced on a small scale in previous periods, but with the Uruk period metallurgy underwent a true explosion. This marks the beginning of the 'Bronze Age' according to the old and still useable system of periodization. The basic metal for the production of tools and weapons was copper, at first by itself or with the addition of some other elements, especially arsenic. Then the definitive choice was made to alloy copper with tin for the production of bronze, and that choice marked the Uruk period. The equipment needed for the fusion is not very sophisticated: an oven, crucibles, moulds, and little else. In fact, this work had already been done before the urban revolution. It continued to be practiced later on, both in central and domestic spheres, in settings that were quite modest.

There were three real problems: the supply of minerals which were obtained through long distance trade, the availability of fuel, much less abundant in Lower Mesopotamia than in the mountain and woodland peripheries, and finally, technical know-how. Because of the need for transport and fuel, a major part of the productive process was located in or near the zones of origin of the minerals. The minerals were moulded into metal ingots that were transported. Sometimes even the finished objects were produced there. But the final production could also take place in Lower Mesopotamia. Copper ingots arrived there first from Oman in the south, later also from Anatolia and Cyprus in the west. Tin ingots were imported from Afghanistan. On the whole, the procurement of metals favored a central organization, palace or temple, controlling the trade. The need for technical know-how, which used to be transmitted within the family workshop, forced the central agency to acquire full-time labor. Smiths were specialists who were supported by the administration through the methods already discussed. They were kept to manufacture commissioned objects, whose quantities depended on the amounts of minerals given to them. The administrative records kept account of the waste from the metal during manufacture, using standard percentages. The destination of the finished products was also to a large extent public. Private demand was satisfied through the 'mixed' procedure, that is, marginal production on the part of palace specialists. The whole centralization of metallurgy did thus not depend much on the sophistication of the productive technology, but more on factors of supply and demand.

The same was true for the production with luxury metals, silver and gold, and for work with semi-precious stones. The long-distance supply of precious materials and the prestige of this type of workmanship brought about a centralization of craftsmen in the ranks of the public administration. Any possible needs at the family level were satisfied through the 'mixed' procedure. The 'duplicate' system, with manufacture both in the family and the temple, prevailed instead in work with materials that were not prestigious and had widespread use. Those included, for instance, work with non-exotic woods for furniture and tools, and the weaving of wicker and other vegetal fibers for containers and mats.

Therefore, artisans on the whole remained to various degrees distributed between the public and the private sectors, between the redistributive system and local exchange. The advent of a central organization of crafts depended more on the growth of needs than on strictly technological problems. The inclusion of a vast and particularized array of specialists with full-time employment in the ranks of the central agency did not exclude the more modest, but widespread, needs of the population which continued to support forms of decentralized labor and part-time work.

5. *Services: Who Serves Whom?*

The service sector on the whole has to be considered in two distinct parts. We have already seen how the development of a central agency on the model of the 'household', required an empowering, if only quantitatively, of domestic services that on a small scale had already characterized the family unit: that is, the preparation of food and clothing. The temples and palaces gathered groups of women for different tasks. Large groups were used as millers and weavers. Smaller groups were set to work in the kitchen, to bake, to maintain buildings, and to give daily provisions to full-time staff and corvée workers. It is probable that the compulsory work originally had a somewhat ceremonial aspect to it. Such an idea survives in royal inscriptions of the second and first millennia, where feeding was done according to the laws of hospitality. The ceremonial aspect weakened quite early on, because of the great concentration of workers. In the central agencies, hospitality modeled after the private sphere remained an issue only when strangers passed through, that is, messengers, merchants, and envoys from other palaces. Under the laws of hospitality these were supplied with food and drink, clothing and balms.

The sector of domestic services was centered inside the 'great households', and only meant the reinforcement of practices in use in normal houses. But, the advent of urbanization and a centralized administration generated another and larger complex of services. These services were essentially new and principally involved contacts with the outside, that is, the population of the early state. The services were connected to defense, the cult, and administration. The last two require a longer discussion that will be developed in §§ 1 and 2 of the next chapter. In the protection from dangers and outside attacks, two different needs must be distinguished. A permanent service of guards was needed for the palace, the storerooms, and the city gates. These had to be protected every night and day by specialized guard personnel, who were supported by the temple or the palace, and usually remunerated with rations or with plots of land. Furthermore, an armed corps was needed in the case of war. For logistical reasons wars only took place in the summer season, and they were not necessarily frequent. They were conducted with armies levied through military corvée, using the same mechanisms as we have already discussed for seasonal manpower, in agriculture and construction. The central agency paid for the maintenance of the soldiers with rations, and provided the necessary tools, in this case weapons. The social costs (including casualties and invalidities) fell on the communities from which the soldiers originated.

This scheme was valid for all of Mesopotamian history, but – in truth – it is not easily documented for the Uruk period. There are attestations of guards in the central administration, but war is documented only in the iconographic material, which is mostly of a celebratory and ideological nature. Notwithstanding this poverty of documentation, there is no doubt that the Late Uruk army was based on corvée duty: there was no alternative.

This solution to the problems of protection leads us to doubt that there was a truly generalized service, available to the total population. The full-time service of guards was unmistakably intended to protect the conspicuous concentration of wealth, which stemmed from the central storage of agricultural goods in magazines, the influx of luxury goods in craft workshops, and the collection and display of temple furnishings. In normal times the guards protected the central wealth *from* the population. They did not protect *the* population, except for the fact that the maintenance of public order is to the advantage of all. Just as indicative is the construction of defensive walls. In the Late Uruk period these began to characterize cities and differentiate them from villages. In the case of an attack, it was technically impossible to defend the agro-pastoral territory and its population. Defense was thus limited to the concentrations of movable wealth, specialized knowledge, and symbolic value that resided in or around the temples.

Mobilization in the case of war was more a service required of the general population than a service provided to them. This observation is clearly valid only on the economic and the organizational level. But, in more general terms, we should not exclude the possibility that the population responded to mobilization with enthusiastic participation. But this depended both on the level of ideological motivation throughout the communities of the early state (we will return to this point in § 2 of the next chapter), and on the specific circumstances of the war. A defensive war is usually more acceptable than an offensive one; a war against foreign barbarians is more acceptable than one against neighbors, and so on.

Chapter 4

POLITICS AND CULTURE OF THE EARLY STATE

1. *The Scribe and the Administration of the Storage House*

The first true and proper system of writing appeared at Uruk in level IV of the Eanna precinct. It appeared on small clay tablets, onto which 'pictographic' signs were incised with a reed stylus to represent numbers, objects, proper names, and titles. In the following level III, the system underwent slight formal changes. When new texts appeared at Ur in the Early Dynastic II period, the signs had assumed their characteristic 'cuneiform' aspects that would remain typical of all later Mesopotamian script. The archaic texts of Uruk IV–III were administrative in nature and were clearly connected with the administration of the economy by the central agencies. They were retrieved in archaeological discharges of the temple area. Some texts were of a lexical character, the sign lists; they were mnemonic aids in the training of scribes.

The archaeological sequence at Susa has provided the most useful evidence in the study of the origins of writing. It shows an earlier use of seals stamped on 'bullae', that is, pieces of clay that sealed the locks of doors and the openings of portable containers. Also used were tokens of clay or stone, symbolizing a physical entity such as a person, animal, or object, and numerical signs. We see the following sequence at Susa. First, tokens were included in bullae of clay, covered with seal impressions. Then the tokens placed inside were imprinted on the exterior of the bullae. Finally, the inclusion of the tokens was abandoned, because the outside impressions, as well as the numerical signs, sufficed to transmit the necessary information (Fig. 10). In this last stage the form of the bulla was flattened, and the 'tablet' shape originated. It is evident that certain non-pictographic, but symbolic, signs (such as that for sheep) derived their form from the tokens with the same meaning. The greater flexibility of the graphic system as compared to the objectual system, however, allowed a transition from a very limited repertory of tokens to a repertory of graphic signs that numbered in the hundreds.

If the derivation of the script from tokens seems undeniable, there are conceptual and historical problems with accepting another observation by some scholars. They argue that writing has very ancient origins, from well before the urban revolution, because tokens and seals are attested already in the seventh millennium BCE. Indeed, the use of seals and tokens had ancient origins in the Neolithic period, but it responded then to needs that were very different from those of the early urban society. This use, which remained constant for four millennia, did not give rise to writing. Instead, it was re-employed to give birth to writing at the moment when new conditions and needs came into existence.

In its Neolithic use the seal undoubtedly identified the person who carried it by means of its distinctive decoration, which was, at first, geometrical and later also teriomorphic. Initially it must have simply been a personal token, suspended from the neck. It was a sort of personalized mark with varied symbolic uses we should not try to guess, since we cannot document them. When seals started to be used as a means of identity, by pressing them onto soft substances such as mud and clay, the correspondence between the seal and the impression symbolized that between the person and the sealed goods. It referred to the concept of property in a broad sense. Certain 'spindle-shaped bullae' of the Halaf period, for example, could have had a function in the management of flocks. Also the 'plain' tokens, that is, those not differentiated in form, could have served as mnemonic aids only, and for calculations at a personal level. Thus, the Neolithic use of seals and tokens corresponded to the needs of an economy of individual families, without any implication that it led to an impersonal administration. At the most one can think of a situation where a 'guard of the storage house' served more than one family, as, for example, at the site of Sabi Abyad from the Halaf period.

Naturally, the system became more complex when the relations between families gradually intensified, and when social stratification appeared, indicating the emergence of elites and of Chalcolithic chiefdoms. Then, the so-called 'complex' tokens emerged. These had a limited repertory of shapes with distinctive values based on their form, size, and decoration. Also, seals with more individual characteristics in their decorations appeared. Finally, tokens and seals were combined in the bullae. That system responded to the needs of an incipient redistributive economy in the Late Ubaid and Early Uruk periods, with an official juridical sanction of the local exchange of resources.

The rapid evolution in the third quarter of the fourth millennium BCE, illustrated by the sequence at Susa described above, culminated in a system of true writing, which responded to the needs of an impersonal administration in central agencies. The replacement of the stamp seal by the cylinder seal may seem a purely formal fact, but it facilitated the total coverage of a piece of clay with a sealing, which accentuates its function as a juridical and administrative guarantee more than that of a symbolic identification. It also underscores the functional character of the operation itself, rather than the personal one. Furthermore, the fact that the sealings (pieces of clay) did not have to be thrown away immediately after they were broken off, but could be kept for accounting and control purposes (one could say 'kept in an archive' to use a concept proposed by Enrica Fiandra), opened up prospects that went well beyond the needs of the individual family. Seals, quantitative indicators (numbers), and the impressions of tokens (and later, graphic symbols) were all related to each other. Especially when they were applied to independent and conservable documents, which replaced a continuous and repetitive use and remaking of sealings, it demonstrates the autonomous emergence of an administrative archive being kept over long periods of time – besides the still lasting system of guarantee against break-ins of containers and magazines. The new system also shows the existence of periodic controls (annually or with different intervals) and of verification. There is no doubt thus that writing responded to specific needs of the early state administration, apart from its precedents which had other functions and were used in different contexts.

Writing essentially served for the administration of central stores. Those who knew how to write, an activity that rapidly became so complex that it required an exacting training, that is, the scribes, were the same as the administrators. It is true that beside administrative texts, which make up ninety percent of the preserved Uruk IV–III tablets, there were also lexical texts, which make up the remaining ten percent. But those were mostly practical instruments, rather than having an independent purpose.

The concept of the 'management of the storehouse' carried a double level of complexity. At the simplest and most obvious level it assured and confirmed an actual correspondence between the quantities of merchandise that entered and exited the storage house. This concept of inventory would remain constant over time. Also the terminology would not change: there was 'income' and 'expenditure', and the two were compared in the form of a 'balance'. The scribe responsible for a certain store did not only have to restrict access to the stored resources by sealing doors and containers with his own seal, so as to protect them against break-ins and theft, he also had to register on tablets the quantities that entered and exited. In this way he would be able at any moment to state the exact contents of what was stored, and the correct destination of the expenditures. In sum, he knew the entire complex administration of the resources for which he was responsible. The scribe thus did not register just for the sake of memory, as the head of the Neolithic family would have done, but as guarantee before the central administration and the entire community.

On another level, the new administration dealt with the relations of transformation and exchange. These can also be reduced to a balance between acquisitions and expenditures, even if the operations are conceptually more complex. For example, a scribe could register the goods that were entrusted to a merchant when he left on a trade journey. That allowed a comparison with the value of the goods the merchant brought back six months later. Or he could register the composition of a flock entrusted to a shepherd. So a year later he would be able to control whether the same flock had grown by the standard rate, and whether the wool and dairy accounts were accurate. Or, he could register the harvest estimate of a field owned by the temple. So he would be able to arrange for the personnel needed to work the field, and he could later check that the barley delivered was indeed two-thirds of the total harvest. All these – and other – operations were not just records of the merchandise coming in and going out. They calculated and converted the value of one merchandise into the value of another merchandise, or the value of goods into labor. They calculated production quotas per unit of labor time, and accounted for rations differentiated by sex, age, function, and so on. This complex of operations can be reduced conceptually to an 'inventory of the storage house', but it shows the superior and incomparable complexity of a storage house in the sphere of the central administration, with its multiple processes of transformation and compensation involving diverse sectors. In comparison, the storage house in the family sphere was a simple place of deposit with entries and expenditures of the same goods.

In the end, there was a temporal delay when some operations remained unfinished, sometimes even for many months, and these were guaranteed by their registration on tablets, as in an inventory. This led to proper archives. The basic registration of single operations came to be abstracted in monthly or annual summaries. Sometimes accounts covering several years were created. The establishment of such secondary registers or summaries made it possible to discard the majority of small basic registrations from the archive. An archive was alive: documents were entered, conserved, and eliminated according to their function as guarantee of administrative operations. They were not archived forever to serve for future recollection for statistical purposes. So our understanding of a single document has to be guided by a reasonable comprehension of the complex procedural mechanism of which it was a functional element.

2. *The Sexagesimal World*

We have mentioned already the introduction of standardized measures to indicate the values of merchandise, rations and so on, needed to subject them to administrative control. Scribal administration had quite a heavy impact on how the real world was seen, certainly more than scholars usually assume. Our knowledge of the ancient reality is distorted to a degree by the administrative filter, but we should not forget that the ancient perception of reality was also largely influenced by the necessity of computing and cataloguing.

A first level of standardization of reality derives from the inventory itself of its constitutive parts. The lexical lists – instruments that helped scribal activity – contain in fact a taxonomic summary of reality. In the infinite variability of the real, typological or functional units were fixed through their relationship to economic use. This taxonomy became even stricter and more functional in the administrative texts. For example, in the range of forms and dimensions of vessels a set of types and standard capacities was established. That made it possible both to standardize the potters' productivity, and, especially, to assign specific uses to different types of vessels. The taxonomic standardization influenced reality itself, by making the capacity of containers coincide with the standard measures. Another example: the stages in the life of a sheep were articulated through specifications that were useful in annual accounting, where sheep still alive were distinguished from those deceased after the last control. The principal concern was to calculate productivity. A female sheep can give birth, a ram cannot; a female produces milk, a male does not; a male produces more wool than a female. Furthermore, an adult sheep is one that is old enough to produce offspring, a young sheep is one that cannot produce now, but will be likely to do so next year. Administratively an adult sheep gives birth to one lamb every two years, and will alternate the sexes of its offspring. And so on.

It was essential to calculate the time and amount of labor, both to requisition finished products and to proceed to their payment. Labor time was calculated in man-days, that is, the amount of labor one man must perform in a day. This abstraction made it possible to register 'half a man', that is, half a day of labor. The man-day unit was used in relation to amounts of earth to be dug, surfaces of fields to be harvested, or numbers of vessels or textiles to be produced. All these elements in turn were measured according to fixed administrative parameters that intended to strike a balance between the variations appearing in reality. Rations were calculated using the parameters of sex (male/female), age (adult/child), rank, and level of specialization. The differences in the amounts issued depended on the type of ration issued: barley rations were connected to bodily weight (that is, in a standard, administrative weight), and were thus greater for a man than for a woman; oil rations were fixed per individual; and wool rations differed between adults and children, but were the same for men and women. All the numerical relations, both within the ration system and between amounts of rations and labor, strived for simplification in the calculations. They based themselves on proportions that were rounded off and followed the sexagesimal system in use at the time.

The computation of time was also strongly determined by administrative needs, and had a clear sexagesimal structure. It was not simple to determine the exact length of a 'real' solar cycle, or a year, through prolonged astronomical observation. Moreover, it was clear that the solar year did not coincide with the lunar year and the months. Administratively a sexagesimal calendar was introduced, with a year of three hundred and sixty days, subdivided into twelve months of thirty days each. This greatly facilitated scribal computation, but was rough in its approximation of the real astronomical cycle. The discrepancy was compensated by inserting five or six days at the end of the year. Presumably those were feast days, exactly because they were outside the administrative computation of labor.

The administrative organization of space depended on linear measures. The names of those measures show that they were based on human body parts, such as the thumb and the forearm, or on actual measuring instruments, such as the cane. Once the measure derived from the forearm was standardized with a reasonable approximation of the body part (with a value that in 'our' system is close to half a meter), the other measures were established through multiplication and division, using the relationships of 1:10, 1:6, and 1:60. This was done so that it was possible to calculate area and volume in the head – obviously by scribes who had a sexagesimal frame of mind! Although measures of volume were closely related to linear and surface measures, they acquired a scale of their own. They were based on the 'liter', especially used to compute the volume of quantities of barley.

This way it became easy to accomplish complex administrative operations. One could establish the relationship between such diverse elements as the size of a field, weight of barley, quantity of manpower, labor time, and its remuneration. This could be done mentally or with the help of an elementary abacus. Naturally, if any standardization of measurements already causes a reduction to median values, the sexagesimal standardization caused an even greater divergence from reality. It is legitimate to think that the difference would not have been at the administration's expense.

The influence of administrative convention on reality was particularly evident in the systematization of agricultural space. It gave rise to a true and proper 'sexagesimal landscape'. The fields were measured using lengths and surfaces preferentially concentrated on 'rounded' numbers. Furrows were located one cubit apart, and seed was sown with one grain per thumb-measure. The flow of irrigation water was set at 'rounded' times or volumes, and the canals had standardized dimensions in order to calculate the labor needed to dig them. Also in construction projects measures based on the cubit and its multiples prevailed, both when making plans, and for computing the numbers of bricks to be produced and to be put in place. This applied both to volume and labor-time.

Parallel to the standardization of these measures, there was one of weights, especially to calculate amounts of wool, metals, and semi-precious stones. The system was based on a trio of shekel, mina, and talent, and possibly could be anthropomorphic in origin – the talent of thirty kilograms is the load a man can carry. But, above all, it was structured by the sexagesimal sequence 1:60:360. Connected to weights and measures was the calculation of the value of various goods. This was the most subjective system of all, both because the linking of values between different commodities inevitably is conventional, and because true value depends on quality and varies over time. The needs of the administration brought about the preservation of extremely stable conventional relations that span the entirety of Mesopotamian history: one shekel of silver = three hundred liters of barley = twelve liters of sesame oil = six or ten minas of wool = two or three minas of copper.

This standardized, sexagesimal, world is evidently a false reality, because of its simplified typologies and conventional relations. The artificiality directly depended on the needs of the centralized and impersonal administration, and brought about a true revolution in the mental perception of reality, which was just as relevant as that derived from the introduction of writing.

3. *The House of God*

Despite its much larger dimensions and complexity, the 'great organization' (central agency) was envisioned on the model of the small productive unit in the family context. The temple was simply the 'house of god' (in Sumerian *é* and a divine name), and the palace was the 'great house' (in Sumerian *é.gal*). It is clear that another frame of reference did not exist in the cultural perception of the time. The similitude did not end with the simple denomination, however. The administrative elite of the temple organization and of the entire city-state that grew around it, with that elite constituting the political leadership, considered itself as the management of a large 'agricultural farm', owned by the god. Just as in a farm there was a residence for the owner, the temple was the earthly residence of the god. In the city there were also residences for the servants, that is, the administrators and employees of various ranks and grades. There were storerooms for materials and reserves of food, workshops and work areas – exactly as in a normal domestic *oikos*, but on an abnormal scale. Also the presence of slave manpower and the use of day and seasonal laborers paralleled relations that presumably existed on a smaller scale at the level of the family as well.

This model was to a large degree ideological. The earliest scholars of Sumerian administrative texts at the start of the twentieth century accepted it as real, however, and reproduced it in totalizing terms. That is how they developed the theory of the Sumerian 'temple-city', which in the first place refers to the Early Dynastic period, but can easily be projected onto the earlier periods. It portrayed a city where the temple owned all the land, exploited one part of it directly while utilizing the rest as allocations to its dependents. In the temple-city all the people depended on the temple both economically and politically. In it the temple directed all economic activity, that is, production, transformation, and exchange. The evidence that led to this totalizing view was in fact made up of (debatable) projections from a documentation that not only was inadequate, but, above all, unbalanced. All the archives used were temple archives. We know now that small family businesses did not need archives, and thus did not transmit data of similar weight.

It was only in the 1960s that especially the work of Igor Diakonoff put into serious doubt the idea of total dependence on the temple. He re-examined quantitative and terminological data and provided a different picture, in which village communities and extended families had their own roles and importance. Diakonoff's critique was a point of departure for a whole series of ever further revisions. These were inspired by reactions against pre-World War II statism, and by the preference for a more open society. Today it is commonly accepted that the temple-city theory was without foundation, and that the economic role of the temple was limited and balanced by that of the private sector. Scholars agree that, if a state-dominated economy ever developed, it happened only at the end of the third millennium under the Third Dynasty of Ur. With respect to the Uruk period, some of this scholarship ended up contesting that the great buildings of the sacred Eanna precinct were really temples. Instead it proposed that these were ceremonial buildings for communal meals or for other activities, clearly reminiscent of ethnographic parallels. This ignores all evidence from the textual documentation, however, and the continuity between the Uruk and Early Dynastic periods.

In all probability the reasonable view lies in the middle of these two extremes. The role of the temple, both economic and political, was dominant when compared to that of other sectors of society, but the latter had their own space and importance. When we describe Venice in the sixteenth century as a 'mercantile city', or Manchester in the nineteenth century as an 'industrial city', we certainly do not want to assert that their entire populations were dedicated to commerce or employed in factories. We indicate that commerce and industry had pre-eminent roles, and that they were focal points to which other activities referred back. They also influenced political choices to a great extent. I believe that it is possible to state in the same way that the early Sumerian city was a temple-city. I mean this in the sense that the temple played a central role, both in the overall productive structure and in the strategies of decision-making.

The continued existence of village communities and productive family units alongside the temples was guaranteed by the nature of the system described here. The ability of the temple to accumulate surplus was based on exploiting the family sector, more by demanding its labor than by requiring contributions from it. And this continued existence automatically also guaranteed the survival of relations of another nature besides the burdensome redistributive system: the local exchange of products and services, in the form of barter or even of a profit-seeking 'market', and strategies of self-sufficiency. Outside the central administrative and bureaucratic apparatus, legal issues and the regulation of community affairs remained entrusted to collective organisms (assemblies, elders).

The 'great house' of the god, and later of the king, rose above the multiple private 'small houses'. The relations between the great and the small houses – in contrast to the relations that already existed between the latter – were of an unequal nature. A supply of labor in one direction replaced the reciprocal exchange of contributions. There was little or no compensation at all in the form of services that were mostly of an ideological nature. The structural inequality of social functions and of relations, directed to the center, generated a clear social stratification. This was much more accentuated in the public than in the private sector, at least on the higher levels. It completely privileged the temple over the rest of the population. The stratification depended on access to resources and to the decision-making process; it was not set in law. Indeed, from the juridical point of view, the basic population was considered to be 'free', in as much as it owned its means of production (land and livestock). Meanwhile the dependents of the temple were 'servants' of the god, just as later the de-pendents of the palace would be 'servants' of the king, and were devoid of means of production. In a characteristic reversal, the 'free person' was superior to the 'servant', but the 'servant of the god' or the 'servant of the king' was superior to the free. The latter were closer to the center of power, on the ideological level as well as in the concrete ability to enrich themselves.

The archaic state – at least in the model of the urban revolution as attested in Lower Mesopotamia – was in essence a redistributive state with two concentric circles, an inner and an outer one. The inner circle of dependents of the central agency extracted from the outer circle a surplus of labor and, through it, of production. That enabled the support of specialists and the maintenance of the administrative machinery. The inner dependents were fully integrated in the redistributive system, both by giving and by receiving. They provided their services, and received their maintenance in exchange. On the other hand, the outer circle of the 'free' population, gave its contributions to the central agency, receiving practi-cally nothing in exchange. The redistributive system functioned therefore in an unbalanced way: the principal flow went from the outer circle to the central storeroom, and from there, to the inner dependents.

In other words, we can probably say that the archaic state included two categories of subjects. In the outer band, which was the larger one in size, lived people who were subjects in the political and, especially, the fiscal sense. But they were economically free. People in the inner nucleus, on the other hand, depended on the state both politically and for their labor. They were totally integrated in the state-organization that supported itself by exploiting the people in the outer band.

4. *Ideological Mobilization*

Inevitably the extraction of resources, upon which the complex society was based, was painful. It could not realize itself without the use of factors that transcended the natural tendency to self-sufficiency and self-reproduction.

Those would range from physical coercion to ideological persuasion. They focused on a higher interest, which was not immediately visible to the single individual – that is, the comprehensive development of the system. The unequal access to resources between various groups, and the imbalance between giving and receiving, must have been the principal problem that confronted the emerging state, to a degree much greater than in an egalitarian society.

As was the situation in numerous other cases, state formation in Lower Mesopotamia came with a religious ideology. The basic reason is obvious: the extraction of resources was less painful if it was done for the benefit of a super-human entity, endowed with superior powers and with functions that were essential for the survival of the community, than if it was done for the direct benefit of a chief, whom all could see to be a human like everyone else. This religious ideology found its concretization in the enormous and prestigious temple buildings that are archaeologically visible. It is sufficient here to mention the sacred Eanna precinct at Uruk, to take an example from the central core, or the temple complex of Arslantepe, to take an example from the distant periphery.

Texts of the period do not adequately document the specific details of this religious ideology. They are of an administrative character and do not transmit information of an ideological nature. We need to make use of texts from later periods, obviously choosing those texts and themes that most likely reflect conceptions developed earlier on.

First of all, it should be noted how the urban revolution, with its increased labor specialization, was reflected in the emergence of a polytheistic religion. Religiosity that focused on the single problem of reproduction, be it by humans, animals, or plants, was more suited to a Neolithic society. With the urban revolution an entire pantheon was conceptualized, which was internally structured along the lines of human relations of kinship, hierarchy, and functional specialization. In short, there was one god to supervise each type of activity: one for agriculture, one for herding, one for writing, one for medicine, and so on. All gods collaborated, whatever be their rank. Also their decision-making structure was clearly anthropomorphic in character. It had a supreme deity and a divine assembly. This assembly did not refer back to an assumed stage of pre-monarchical primitive democracy (as was stated in the famous theory by Thorkild Jacobsen), but to the everlasting assemblies with local jurisdiction.

In this polytheistic structure, to the general population the divine world in all its complexity remained primarily responsible for the athmospheric phenomena (bringing prosperity or ruin) and for health and reproductive capacities of humans and animals. A large part of the cultic calendar and the ceremonial cycle was based on the agricultural and pastoral year. Also the basic concept of 'sacrifice' or offering without a doubt retained in the minds of the general population the idea of reciprocity, with the returns increased according to rank. The people offered various samples of their products to the gods in order to induce them, encourage them, we could even say 'compel' them, to reciprocate with bountiful harvests and off-spring using the rules of exchange.

The mechanism of offerings functioned thus as a symbolic sublimation of the more generalized mechanism of centralized redistribution. In parallel terms, it is possible that the labor contributions originally had a certain festive character, or at least, that they were conceptually inserted in established customs of labor exchange between different family units. There was an obvious imbalance because the 'house of the god' had a higher rank than the ordinary houses. In the case of products, the imbalance of roles and ranks seems to confirm the idea of augmented return (*noblesse oblige*). In the case of labor, however, it seems to show the idea of non-reciprocation (*droit du seigneur*), unless the reciprocation takes place on other levels and in different forms, such as protection, health, goodwill, and the like.

Other than providing a religious justification for the imbalance of con-tributions, Sumerian ideology seems particularly directed at affirming the positive value of complementary social roles. Manifestations of this are found especially in wisdom literature and mythological texts, both of which are characteristically very conservative and thus presumably go back to a very early period.

The simplest and most ancient examples of wisdom texts are collections of proverbs. The oldest collections are already attested in the middle of the third millennium BCE. They include proverbs like, 'the outer villages maintain the central city' and 'the small city raises livestock for its king, the large city constructs the temple and digs the canal'. Those clearly reflect the hierarchical landscape of Lower Mesopotamia. Other proverbs state, for example, 'Don't drive out the powerful, don't destroy the wall of defense', referring to the need for protection as a justification for the leading elite.

Still more typical are the 'debate poems' where two different, or better opposite, elements or persons confront one another in order to demon-strate the necessity of both. In some cases the interaction was between two elements of equal value. That is true for the debates between ewe and wheat, between herdsman and farmer, and between summer and winter. The poems want to affirm the idea that parallel functions must cooperate rather than compete in order to exist. In other cases the interaction had a strikingly more consolatory undertone, as in the debates between silver and copper, between date palm and tamarisk, and between plow and hoe. Clearly, the two elements are not equal on the level of prestige, but the texts affirm that even the humbler element has its own usefulness, equal to that of the more esteemed and showy element. Likewise, in human society, everyone should be content with his or her tasks, even with the most humble ones. They acquire a value equal to other tasks, because they are all integrated in a complex mechanism where nothing can function without one of these elements.

The myths delineate mental maps that are very directly anchored in the reality of the Lower Mesopotamian landscape, especially those myths dealing with creation. As an example, one can think of the myth of Ninurta, who looks after the entirety of Mesopotamia as if it were an agricultural field. The Tigris and Euphrates rivers act as irrigation canals and the mountain ranges are embankments to hold back the otherwise disastrous floods. Or, one can think of the Lagash King List, which imagines that the human species germinated from the earth after the flood, exactly like plants sprout after irrigation. Of more evident social significance is the myth of Atramhasis. In it humanity is created with the specific function of replacing the minor gods in their hard work of irrigation and cultivation, and of producing for the great gods the food that does not grow in sufficient quantities without labor. That concept perfectly sums up the entire productive condition of Lower Mesopotamia. In various myths and hymns the hoe and the basket become instruments of prestige in the hands of gods and kings. They are the typical labor tools of the workers with the most burdensome corvée tasks of digging and moving earth.

Other mental maps have to do with the relations between the center and the periphery. The most recurrent are those that contrast nomads to sedentary people and the alluvium to the mountains. The pastoral people of the steppe (the Martu) and of the mountains (the Guti) are characterized by the very absence of the most basic traits of urban culture. They have no houses, they have no tombs, they do not know agriculture, and they do not know the rites of cult. It is an ethnocentric vision that aims to strengthen the self-esteem of those living in a world that is culturally superior, but that is potentially threatened by the insistent and violent pressures of foreign peoples. The other recurrent mental map sees each of the mountain ranges around Mesopotamia as holding a typical product, such as a type of tall tree, metal, or stone. Those remain unused there, but are available for the center of the world. Access to them is facilitated by the

Chapter 5

CENTER AND PERIPHERY

1. *The Regional System*

Striking differences appear when we compare the territorial extent of the
Uruk culture with that of the preceding Ubaid culture. The Ubaid culture
embraced all of Mesopotamia, while cultural elements resembling it reached
parts of the Syrian and Anatolian periphery as well. There was thus a wide
horizon of cultural homogeneity. In contrast, the Uruk culture as a phenomenon was restricted to Lower Mesopotamia. Only secondarily, was it
accompanied by episodes of 'colonization', as we see in certain sites of the
Susiana plain and the middle Euphrates Valley. The technological and
organizational development of Uruk was so great that it by far left behind
the late Chalcolithic cultures surrounding it. The widespread homogeneity
of the Ubaid culture was replaced by diversity and complementarity.

This double aspect – the specificity of the Uruk culture and its complementarity with the surrounding cultures – has inspired scholars to use
the concept of a 'world system' when discussing this period of earliest
urbanization. Immanuel Wallerstein developed the 'world system' theory
to refer to the modern era, the period from the great European explora-
tions to the development of colonialism. Its application to a period so
remote in time has given rise to much criticism, above all among scholars
who privilege the importance of local factors in development over the role
of interaction. Moreover, even keeping account of Wallerstein's own
qualification that a 'world system' does not encompass the entire world,
the restricted territorial extension of the Uruk phenomenon may make it
advisable to use the less binding term of 'regional system'.

Whatever term is adopted, there are essentially two problems that
confront the use of the world system model. First, one can ask whether
the interactions between different regions in the Uruk period were so
strong that they characterized and conditioned the processes in itself.
Second, one can ask whether the developments in the Lower Mesopotamian center were related to, and indeed made possible by, parallel

processes of underdevelopment in the periphery, the provider of raw materials. The concept of underdevelopment, as formulated by Gunder Frank, Eric Wolf and others, always with reference to modern colonialism, seems to me a more useful point of reference than Wallerstein's model of the world system.

The ecological complexity of the Near East is well known. Its pattern of precipitation is determined by the fact that two rainfall systems are demarcated in the region. Winds in the easterly direction have an Atlantic origin and bring winter rains. Winds in the north-westerly direction have a monsoonal origin and bring summer rains. The vegetation shows the convergence of various zones: the 'Mediterranean' zone in Anatolia and Syria-Palestine, the 'Turanian' zone in Iran and Central Asia, and the so-called 'Ethiopian' zone in East Africa and Yemen, stretching as far east as the Indus Valley. The mountain ranges along the seacoasts create belts with very different amounts of rainfall in close proximity to one another. The soil types are likewise diverse and close together, with a basic distinction between the river alluviums and the surrounding mountains.

This ecological heterogeneity creates a diversity of regions, each with a very different economic potential and close to each other. There are numerous possibilities of economic activity. They include irrigation agriculture and rain-fed agriculture, animal husbandry in the steppes and in the mountains, the exploitation of woods in the mountains and of marshes in the lowlands, and so on. Agriculture is only possible in restricted areas. In other regions people need to rely on a subsistence strategy of gathering and hunting (including fishing and bird catching). In general terms, as already pointed out for long distance trade, it is important to underline the fundamental complementarity between the alluvial zones, with dense human populations and intensive food production, and the mountain zones, with rich natural resources (wood, metal, and stone).

Already in the context of the pre-urban economies this close proximity of zones with different economic potentials led to systems of complementary use. One just needs to think of the vertical transhumance on the slopes of the Taurus and Zagros mountains, or better still of the seasonal pattern of winter farming and summer grazing in the valley of the Euphrates River. With the Uruk period, the advent of long fields and planned irrigation created an additional economic landscape, limited to the so-called delta region, at first without visibly changing interregional relations. What led to the restructuring of these relations, was the development of great urban agglomerations and the emergence of new needs.

It can be said therefore that the prime mover of urbanization and state formation can be found in the distinctive basic resources available in the

microenvironment of the Lower Mesopotamian delta. This microenvironment built around itself, so to speak, a regional system, according to the
location of additional secondary resources. Some resources were present
or grown locally: they ranged from barley to dates, clay to bitumen, and
reed to fish. Other resources were available in the immediately surrounding area: these included especially sheep and goats. For still others, one had
to maintain contacts over long distances. A large inventory of different
resources was necessary to satisfy the complex needs of the archaic state,
so their dispersed availability was an inconvenience. The variegated landscape of 'greater Mesopotamia' was a positive factor only to the extent that
the interfaces between different ecological zones were close enough.

The location of resources determined then in large measure the destiny
of the various zones (zones of concentrated or dispersed settlement, zones
of archaic states or of residual chiefdoms, etc.), and their combination in a
comprehensive 'regional system'. And here arises the second question
posed at the beginning of the chapter: did the development of the city and
the state at Uruk and its appropriation of resources from the periphery,
force a form of underdevelopment on that same periphery?

The answer certainly should not be ideological or theoretical, but must
be based on the available documentary data. And these data suggest a
negative answer: the cantonal units of the periphery underwent a parallel
development that seems to have been stimulated rather than stymied by
the exchange with Uruk, even if that exchange certainly was unequal. If
these regions took a different path – that is, they became chiefdoms rather
than states – it is due to their own original conditions rather than to interregional relations. Let us posit the hypothetical case of a mountain zone in
a mineral-rich region. That cannot be suitable terrain for a city to develop.
The population supports itself with local agro-pastoral resources, on which
interregional exchange has no influence. The inhabitants of the distant city
in the archaic state see it as a place to acquire metal, and visit the peripheral area only to exploit this resource. The local headmen organize the
labor and in return acquire the prestige goods that reinforce their special
status within their own communities. In sum, there is an incentive for
political and organizational centralization, without specific damage to the
local economy.

It is certain that, in the period of concern here, the economic exploitation of periphery by the center did not involve the basic goods of
consumption, and therefore did not affect the living standards of the
population. Instead, the economic exploitation pertained to resources that
were of a secondary character only. The production and preparation of

these resources was expanded by the appearance of new distant outlets, in addition to the pre-existent and restricted local ones. Even if the wealth derived from this was, in truth, modest when compared to the real 'market'-value of the exported merchandise, it contributed to an increase in the local socio-economic stratification, and it strengthened the elite's hold over general population. It certainly did not lead to a decrease in the total income available to these communities.

Finally, it is necessary to point out, at least in passing, the problem of internal complexity as it affected the microenvironment of Lower Mesopotamia. In the 1960s Robert Adams proposed that the co-existence of diverse economic activities (agriculture and horticulture, pastoralism, fishing and bird catching), rather than the 'hydraulic' factor, could have caused the rise of redistributive agencies. The picture outlined by Adams is certainly correct. However, the need of interaction between these economic components seems to have been of such a nature and extent that it was possible to deal optimally with it through mechanisms of local exchange, without the mediation of a central agency. The exchange mechanisms already existed in societies with an essentially egalitarian structure, for example, the Ubaid society. It seems to me that the advent of one new component, that is, the long field and the planned irrigation it required, stimulated the new need for a central agency. That agency provided mediation, the mobilization of labor, and administrative control, and increased the inequality in access to the decision-making process and to resources. One can perhaps say that the unequal contributions of labor produced more relevant consequences of organizational changes, than the exchange of complementary products.

2. *Primary and Secondary State Formation*

The choice of Uruk as a privileged case in the study of the origins of state organizations is often motivated by its definite primary character. Being the earliest of all, the process of state formation in Lower Mesopotamia cannot have been inspired by others that were anterior and could have influenced it. The quite more numerous cases of secondary state formation run the risk of not disclosing the primary, essential, and uncontaminated characteristics of the process. They may have been inspired by imitation, and may be a complement or a parasite of a model already existing. When he wanted to undertake a comparative study of state formation that was based on strictly primary cases, Robert Adams limited himself to Mesopotamia and Mesoamerica. Not only were Egypt and the Indus Valley civilization most likely secondary in relation to Uruk, but also even the distant

Chinese case could be suspected of having had connections with the Near East, through indirect contact via Central Asia.

Put this way, the problem sounds again like part of the old diffusionist model, monocentric or more likely bicentric, as there were no contacts between the old and new worlds at the time in question. From an original center the state model became increasingly more widespread, perhaps transforming itself in order to adapt to the diverse conditions encountered in the new regions. Without a doubt, diffusionism contains a good dose of historical truth; we should just think of the diffusion of the industrial revolution, which is extremely well documented. But diffusionism tends to obscure the understanding of original mechanisms. It is in fact difficult to trust and utilize a classification that places a single primary case on one side and hundreds of secondary cases on the other side.

Also, in a more strictly historical sense, the primary case runs the risk of losing a good part of its significance if it is not framed in the context of what happened at least in its immediate surroundings. To assess the value of the strategies adopted, consciously or not, which led to state formation, it is appropriate to consider in parallel those societies that were coeval and nearby but chose other strategies, as well as those that developed into states at other times and under different conditions. In this context, secondary state formation can be better examined without pointing at its chronological posteriority or cultural dependence, but by focusing on the existence of different structural connections with concrete ecological and historical factors.

In this respect we should consider that the concept of 'primitive accumulation' had a clear connection with the cases of primary state formation, that is, those where a new socio-political apparatus was developed from a novel concentration of resources derived from internal productive mechanisms. The secondary cases borrowed certain organizational elements already established elsewhere and did not necessarily have the same trajectory as the primary cases. Nor did they necessarily have to base themselves on the same technological, productive, demographic, and urban conditions.

It is enough to think of what Marcella Frangipane recently described as the characteristics of early state development at Arslantepe. There one finds an urban organization without having a city – a paradox that can be explained exactly in the context of relations between primary and secondary states, or between center and periphery. The already mentioned diversity on a regional scale, with its visible disparity between the alluvial zone, with intensive cereal production and dense human settlement, and the mountain zones, with limited productive and demographic potential but a greater concentration of strategic resources, sets the basis for a more effective use of the concept of secondary state formation. Even if it is impossible here to describe the typical processes of secondary urbanization, it is clear to all that these were completely different from those in the alluvium, and that they did not pass through a process of primitive accumulation.

In brief, the opposition between 'primary' and 'secondary' could be rethought in terms of economic structures, rather than in terms of diachronic relations. We can call 'primary' those cases of urbanization and state formation that based themselves substantially on internal resources, and on the primitive accumulation of agricultural products with which our analysis began. We can call 'secondary' those cases that did not pass through a stage of primitive accumulation of their own, because they exploited an accumulation that came about elsewhere, and secured through it structural contacts based on a complementarity of available resources.

Cases like Egypt and the Indus Valley are in this sense 'primary' without a doubt, irrespective of the importance of Mesopotamian influences on them, which is a matter of debate. The Pharaonic and Harappan states based themselves on resources that were essentially their own. They developed and functioned in a self-sufficient way, without having to rely on the existence of an analogous model already in operation elsewhere. Secondary would be those cases (for example, in eastern Anatolia and in Iran) located in zones that were not alluvial. The problems of the coordination of production with a hydraulic origin were therefore alien to them, and they would not have been able to develop without an earlier primary urbanization to which they could refer.

The more specific cases where we see the diffusion of early state organizational structures are the so-called Late Uruk colonies in the regions of the Middle Euphrates and Upper Mesopotamia. There we can distinguish: (1) true colonies, such as Habuba Kabira, that is, settlements fully within the Late Uruk cultural horizon but located outside the zone where that culture originated; (2) commercial outposts, such as Godin Tepe, which were small and were inserted in centers with a predominant indigenous culture; (3) indigenous centers, such as Arslantepe, which were influenced on the organizational level by the Late Uruk model. Although there were essential differences, in all these cases the early urban model with a central organization and impersonal administration took root, not to confront local problems of administering primary production, but to deal with problems of the exchange of different resources on a regional scale.

Many aspects remain to be clarified, also with regard to more recently obtained data. We can cite once more the example of Arslantepe: the discovery that the Late Uruk period temple complex, clearly influenced by the Uruk culture, was located on an earlier Late Chalcolithic complex, which was already monumental, poses an interesting problem that can be clarified only with an increase of available data. At the moment two explanations are legitimate: either the Late Chalcolithic complex, which was contemporaneous with the Early Uruk period, already followed the model of Lower Mesopotamia, or indigenous development was strong enough to cause important processes of organizational restructuring before the intensification of relations with the Lower Mesopotamian world. One can even propose an explanation with two stages: first, there was a process of a primary nature, rather modest because of the limited extent of the local territory; then a secondary process arose out of this, when it became embedded into the regional system hinged upon Uruk. 'Primary' and 'secondary' are in the end analytical instruments and not factual realities.

3. *The Problem of Collapse*

At the height of its development the Late Uruk culture included the following elements: a capital of indisputable preeminence, Uruk itself measuring one hundred hectares, with its sacred and organizational center at the Eanna precinct; a central territory that embraced all of Lower Mesopotamia (poorly known in this phase, unfortunately) and Khuzistan (Susa); a zone that we can define as the semi-periphery, Upper Mesopotamia, with a mixed culture; and a zone with commercial outposts distributed over the Anatolian and Iranian highlands. But this system had a short lifespan of only a couple of centuries. The settlements of the periphery were destroyed or abandoned, and the long development of the Eanna center was interrupted. It seems, therefore, that the first period of urbanization faced a crisis or a real collapse, after a long formative phase and the culmination of its internal organization (writing) and commercial expansion (colonies).

The crisis presents characteristics that are very different between the periphery and the center. In the periphery, where urbanization was quite modest and the administrative apparatus extemporaneous, the collapse was total. A colony such as Habuba Kabira, which had been founded on virgin soil, was fully abandoned. The commercial outposts inserted in indigenous zones, such as Godin Tepe or Hassek Höyük, disappeared, leaving the local settlements to their own fate. Even in Susiana, however close to the central nucleus of Lower Mesopotamia, the Late Uruk interval ended as suddenly as it began. At the opposite end of the Near East, the indigenous center of Arslantepe, with an early state organization, saw the destruction of its Late Uruk period temple complex. It became covered by a village with huts of Transcaucasian shepherds whose chief was buried in a tomb of unparalleled wealth. The tomb almost came to symbolize how the surplus of production could be used very differently, either for social benefits or for personal treasury.

With the collapse of the early state system, the Mesopotamian periphery saw a cultural fragmentation arise, emblematically represented by varied types of pottery. We find hand-made burnished red-black ware of the Transcaucasian horizon, Syro-Anatolian ceramics of reserved slip ware, painted and impressed pottery identified as Upper Mesopotamian Ninevite V, and so on. The settlements were on the level of villages, either agricultural or pastoral. The level of organization must be assumed as having been of the chiefdom type. There were no more indicators of scribal administration, and monumental architecture vanished. A new phase of urbanization, with writing, a central administration, and palaces, would only come about in the second quarter of the third millennium, again due to Lower Mesopotamian influences. That phase would culminate in the Proto-Elamite culture at Susa and in the Ebla culture in northern Syria.

Certainly of lesser importance was the crisis in Lower Mesopotamia. What happened to the sacred Eanna precinct at Uruk was not universal. Settlement data demonstrate that population growth and the rate of urbanization perhaps slowed down somewhat, and that there was a restructuring of the political system. From a single center at Uruk there developed a plurality of equivalent centers. The scribal and administrative traditions demonstrate continuity from the Late Uruk period to the mature Early Dynastic, so it is unthinkable that there was a true and proper hiatus – notwithstanding the scarcity and almost total absence of texts between the Uruk III ones and those of the Early Dynastic II and III periods. Undoubtedly, the Early Dynastic I period (2900–2700 BCE) represents a phase of economic depression and little visible cultural accomplishments. However, the impression of continuity seems to prevail over that of discontinuity. Unfortunately, many of our conclusions must be provisional as the documentation is not of a sort to permit certainty.

With necessary prudence we can adopt two alternative interpretations – rather than proper explanations – for the collapse of the Late Uruk culture: either a crisis at the center caused the abandonment of its colonial outposts, or disturbances at the periphery, such as pastoral migrations, provoked a general contraction of the sphere of Uruk's influence. A coincidence of several factors is not excluded. But the different impact of the crises in the center and the periphery must lead in any case to a consideration of general nature. Urbanization in the Lower Mesopotamian core, in the area of irrigation agriculture and especially that of planned irrigation, seems to have been acquired forever, just requiring adjustments in order to be able to become even better. On the other hand, urbanization in the periphery seems to have been a more superficial phenomenon that was inspired by the outside, and was not yet able to take root in the region. Therefore it was open to collapse.

In seeing the modifications that were necessary to overcome the crisis, the following seems to be an important consideration: while the central agencies that propelled the first urbanization had a clear temple-like character, those in the second period of urbanization were more palatial in character. That means that the political functions detached themselves from the temple and were relocated in a building that was 'secular', whatever the religious aspects of the political ideology in the first palaces may have been. In the Lower Mesopotamian core where the system had continuity, temple and palace coexisted in the administration of the economy. The temples had the role of subordinated agencies under the control of the palace. In the periphery, on the other hand, after the phase of institutional regression, the second urbanization became truly palatial and the temples took on only cultic roles. They were loci of redistributive activity of a ceremonial character.

If we push to the limits what can be reasonably documented, we could say that the second urbanization accepted compromise as a solution, whereas the first was a more rigid phase of 'temple revolution'. The emergence of royal powers, that assumed in certain cases a clear militaristic character (Akkad) and in other cases a mercantile character (Ebla), constituted in a certain way a kind of revenge of those kin-based elites that had been set aside by the impersonal administration of the temple institution. The mixed system of temple and palace gave greater satisfaction to the needs of consumption, ostentation, and treasuring by individuals and kin groups, once the oppressive 'primitive accumulation' had established itself in an irreversible form. If we look at the chart outlining the sizes of buildings over time (Diag. 3, p. 23), we can hypothesize that the first palaces carried on the trajectory of growth in private houses for the pre-urban elites – after a hiatus that is only partly documented.

In the periphery, the new and more flexible model showed itself better suited at dealing with an economy that did not depend on planned irrigation, but on a mixture of rain-fed agriculture and pastoral transhumance, with marked components of trade and/or of forest or mineral resources, depending on the region. The requirements of social accumulation of food and social mobilization of labor were less compelling. A great deal of opportunity was left for consumption by the elites, for interactions between clans, and for a social stratification based on personal factors of prestige and wealth, rather than on a position within an impersonal administration.

All in all, the old (temple) model was too strictly functional a solution for the specific problems of the irrigated alluvium. The new model, with its coexistence of palace and temple, could take root in a wider territory, including in the periphery. In fact, the first experiments with urbanization outside the alluvial zones were absolutely secondary, always functioning for the needs of the center. The second period of urbanization, on the other hand, on the plateaus with rain-fed agriculture, and even in mountain regions, gave rise to states that were secondary only in part, and were based both on local resources, and on their integration within a regional structure that continued to have its epicenter (although not exclusively) in the demographic concentrations with cereal agriculture of the major alluvial zones.

It is a fact that urbanization had its costs, economic and especially social. In Lower Mesopotamia surplus production was possible – we can even say easy – because of the fortunate concurrence between ecological and technological conditions and the political and administrative structures. That was more difficult in regions where the cereal yields were only half, or even a third, of those in the irrigated alluvium and where fewer people could be mobilized. In those zones, the early state had either to satisfy itself with more modest social contributions, or else it had to force development to such a limit that it could break. This structural reason remained at the basis of all cycles of urbanization – very visible in the periphery but much less in the alluvium – that characterize the long stretch of Mesopotamian history, with their slow progressions and their more sudden collapses. The extraordinary achievements of the ancient Near East, in architecture and urbanism, arts and letters, technology and ideology, were not the results of miracles, but of the coordination of ingenious technical feats, painful chargings of social labor, and a religious ideology that was very efficient for mobilization. Not always, nor for long periods, did such coordination prevail over the easier trends towards never changing self-consumption and self-reproduction.

BIBLIOGRAPHY

Introduction: *Uruk, the First Complex Society in the Ancient Near East*

For general information on the Uruk period, see M. Frangipane, *La nascita dello Stato nel Vicino Oriente* (Rome-Bari, 1996), ch. 7; H.J. Nissen, *The Early History of the Ancient Near East, 9000–2000 B.C.* (Chicago, 1988), ch. 4. On the basic concepts of the urban revolution, see M. Liverani, *L'origine delle città* (Rome, 1986). On the excavations at Uruk, see H. Lenzen (and others), *Vorläufiger Berichte über die Ausgrabungen in Uruk-Warka* (Berlin, 1930–1972), I-XXVII.

Chapter 1. *History of the Question*

1. *The Urban Revolution and the Legacy of the Nineteenth Century*
The citation from J. Burckhardt was mentioned in M. Liverani's preface to M. Frangipane, *La nascita dello Stato*, p. vii. The quote from V. Gordon Childe is from *What Happened in History* (Harmondsworth: Penguin Books, 1942), pp. 97-101. On Childe, see B. Trigger, *Gordon Childe: Revolutions in Archaeology* (London, 1980) and D.H. Harris (ed.), *The Archaeology of V. Gordon Childe* (Chicago, 1994).

2. *Theories in Conflict: 'Modernists' and 'Primitivists'*
F. Heichelheim, *An Ancient Economic History* (3 vols.; Leiden, 1938). The works of K. Polanyi referred to are *The Great Transformation* (New York, 1944), and *Trade and Market in the Early Empires* (New York, 1957). The idea of 'staple finance' was introduced by K. Polanyi in *Primitive, Archaic, and Modern Economies: Essays of Karl Polanyi* (Garden City, 1968), p. 321.

3. *Neo-evolutionism and Continuity*
The neo-evolutionist vision is stated, for example, by E.R. Service, *Primitive Social Organization* (New York, 1962) and M.H. Fried, *The Evolution of Political Society* (New York, 1967). For general overviews, see H. Claessen and P. Skalnik (eds.), *The Early State* (Paris, 1978); E. Service, *Origins of the State and Civilization* (New York, 1975). For a criticism I refer to N. Yoffee, 'Too Many Chiefs? (or, Save Texts for the '90s)', in N. Yoffee and A. Sherratt (eds.), *Archaeology Today: Who Sets the Agenda?* (Cambridge, 1993), pp. 60-78.

4. *Complexity and Transition*
On the concept of 'complexity' as applied to archaeology and early history, see, among others, S.E. van der Leeuw (ed.), *Archaeological Approaches to the Study of Complexity* (Amsterdam, 1981). On 'complex chiefdoms', see T. Earle, *Chiefdoms: Power, Economy,*

and Ideology (Cambridge, 1991). For its use in ancient Mesopotamia, G. Stein and M.S. Rothman (eds.), *Chiefdoms and Early State in the Ancient Near East: The Organizational Dynamics of Complexity* (Madison,WI, 1994). On the primacy of demographic factors, I refer to E. Boserup, *The Conditions of Agricultural Growth* (Chicago, 1965). On various factors in state formation, see H.T. Wright, 'Recent Research on the Origin of the State', *Annual Review of Anthropology* 6 (1977), pp. 379-97. The use of flow-charts started with C.L. Redman, *The Rise of Civilization* (San Francisco, 1978).

5. *The 'Archaic' Texts from Uruk*
The first edition of 'archaic' texts from Uruk was by A. Falkenstein, *Archaische Texte aus Uruk* (Leipzig, 1936). The re-edition in progress includes M.W. Green and H.J. Nissen, *Zeichenliste der archaischen Texte aus Uruk* (Berlin, 1987). For their use in economic history, H.J. Nissen, P. Damerow and R.K. Englund, *Archaic Bookkeeping: Early Writing and Techniques of Economic Administration in the Ancient Near East* (Chicago, 1993).

Chapter 2. *Social Transformation of the Territory*

1. *Primitive Accumulation and Technical Innovations*
For the concept of the 'hydraulic society' the work of K. Wittfogel, *Oriental Despotism* (New Haven, 1957) remains important, but its political ideology has to be set aside. On the geomorphology of Lower Mesopotamia, P. Sanlaville, 'Considérations sur l'évolution de la Basse Mésopotamie au cours des derniers millénaires', *Paléorient* 15 (1989), pp. 5-27. On the Lower Mesopotamian system of long fields, M. Liverani, 'The Shape of the Neo-Sumerian Fields', *Bulletin on Sumerian Agriculture* 5 (1990), pp. 147-86; 'Reconstructing the Rural Landscape of the Ancient Near East', *Journal of the Economic and Social History of the Orient* 39 (1996), pp. 1-41. On the difference between the 'valley' and the 'delta', M. Liverani, 'Lower Mesopotamian Fields: South vs. North', in *Festschrift für W. Röllig* (Neukirchen, 1997), pp. 219-27. The seeder-plow, B. Hruška, 'Der Umbruchplug in den archaischen und altsumerischen Texten', *Archiv Orientalni* 53 (1985), pp. 46-55 and *Archiv Orientalni* 56 (1988), pp. 137-58. Barley yields, J.N. Postgate, 'The Problem of Yields in Sumerian Texts', *Bulletin on Sumerian Agriculture* 1 (1984), pp. 97-102. The threshing sledge, M.A. Littauer, J.H. Crouwel and P. Steinkeller, 'Ceremonial Threshing in the Ancient Near East', *Iraq* 52 (1990), pp. 15-23; P.C. Anderson and M.L. Inizan, 'Utilisation du tribulum au début du IIIe millénaire', *Paléorient* 20 (1994), pp. 85-103. The secondary revolution, A. Sherratt, 'The Secondary Exploitation of Animals in the Old World', *World Archaeology* 15 (1983), pp. 90-104. Climatic factors, F. Hole, 'Environmental Instability and Urban Origins', in *Chiefdoms and Early State in the Near East* (Madison, WI, 1994), pp. 121-51.

2. *Destination of the Surplus*
On the Ubaid period, see E.F. Henrickson and I. Theusen (eds.), *Upon This Foundation: The 'Ubaid Reconsidered* (Copenhagen, 1989); and G. Stein, 'Economy, Ritual, and Power in 'Ubaid Mesopotamia', in *Chiefdoms and Early State in the Near East* (Madison, WI, 1994), pp. 35-46. The quote from K. Marx is from *Capital*, volume I, part 2 (ed. R. Tucker; *The Marx-Engels Reader* [New York, 2nd edn, 1978], p. 432).

3. *Demography and Settlement*
Site surveys in Lower Mesopotamia, R. McC. Adams, *Land behind Baghdad* (Chicago, 1965); *The Uruk Countryside* (Chicago, 1977); *Heartland of Cities* (Chicago, 1981). For an analysis in the style of the New Geography, G. Johnson, 'Strutture protostatali', *Annali dell'Istituto Orientale di Napoli* 43 (1983), pp. 345-406.

4. *Social Structure*
For the architectural development of the house, O. Aurenche, *La maison orientale* (Paris, 1981). On the presumed Ubaid elites, J.F. Forest, *L'apparition de l'état en Mésopotamie* (Paris, 1996). The evolution of land tenure in Mesopotamia, M. Liverani, 'Land Tenure and Inheritance in the Ancient Near East', in T. Khalidi (ed.), *Land Tenure and Social Transformation in the Middle East* (Beirut, 1984), pp. 33-44, and the contributions by P. Steinkeller (pp. 11-27), H. Neumann (pp. 29-48), and J. Renger (pp. 49-67) in *Das Grundeigentum in Mesopotamien* (*Jahrbuch für Wirtschafsgeschichte*, Sonderband 1987; Berlin, 1988).

Chapter 3. *The Administration of a Complex Economy*

1. *The Cycle of Barley*
The theoretical model used here was adapted from W. Kula, *An Economic Theory of the Feudal System: Towards a Model of the Polish Economy 1500–1800* (New York, 1987). On the Mesopotamian ration system, I.J. Gelb, 'The Ancient Mesopotamian Ration System', *Journal of Near Eastern Studies* 24 (1965), pp. 230-43; L. Milano, 'Le razioni alimentari nel Vicino Oriente antico', in R. Dolce and C. Zaccagnini (eds.), *Il pane del re* (Bologna, 1989), pp. 65-100. For rations in the Uruk period, M. Frangipane, *ibid.*, pp. 49-63.

2. *The Cycle of Wool*
The husbandry of sheep and goats in the Uruk period, M.W. Green, 'Animal Husbandry at Uruk in the Archaic Period', *Journal of Near Eastern Studies* 39 (1980), pp. 1-35; M. Liverani, 'The Uruk Origins of Mesopotamian Administrative Conventions', *Acta Sumerologica* 17 (1995), pp. 127-34. Archaeological data from Arslantepe, S. Bökönyi, 'Late Chalcolithic and Early Bronze I Animal Remains from Arslantepe', *Origini* 12 (1983), pp. 581-98. Wool and linen, J. McCorriston, 'The Fiber Revolution: Textile Extensification, Alienation, and Social Stratification in Ancient Mesopotamia', *Current Anthropology* 38 (1997), pp. 517-49. Textile workshops, K. Maekawa, 'Female Weavers and their Children', *Acta Sumerologica* 2 (1980), pp. 81-125; I.J. Gelb, 'The Arua Institution', *Revue d'Assyriologie* 66 (1972), pp. 1-32.

3. *Commerce: Procurement or Profit?*
The theory of 'administered trade' comes from K. Polanyi, *Trade and Market in the Early Empires* (New York, 1957). On long-distance trade in the Uruk period, H. Weiss and T.C. Young, 'The Merchants of Susa', *Iran* 13 (1975), pp. 1-17. On local exchange, G. Johnson, *Local Exchange and Early State Development in Southwestern Iran* (Ann Arbor, 1973). On Neo-Sumerian annual balanced accounts, D.C. Snell, *Ledgers and Prices: Early Mesopotamian Merchant Accounts* (New Haven, 1982).

4. *Crafts: Centralization or Diffusion?*

For the archaeological visibility of craft specialization, M. Tosi, 'The Notion of Craft Specialization and its Representation in the Archaeological Record', in M. Spriggs (ed.), *Marxist Perspectives in Archaeology* (Cambridge, 1984), pp. 22-52. Specialization in the village community, G.M. Schwartz and S.E. Falconer (eds.), *Archaeological Views from the Countryside* (Washington, 1994). Ceramic production, P. Steinkeller, 'The Organization of Crafts in Third Millennium Babylonia: The Case of Potters', *Altorientalische Forschungen* 23 (1996), pp. 232-53. For ration bowls, A. Le Brun, 'Les écuelles grossières: état de la question', in M.T. Barrelet (ed.), *L'archéologie de l'Iraq* (Paris, 1980), pp. 59-83. Metal alloys from the Uruk period, M. Frangipane, 'Early Development of Metallurgy in the Near East', in *Studi in onore di S. Puglisi* (Rome, 1985), pp. 215-28. Organization of specialized labor, lastly, J. Renger, 'Handwerk und Handwerker im alten Mesopotamien', *Altorientalische Forschungen* 23 (1996), pp. 211-31.

5. *Services: Who Serves Whom?*

The model of the 'household' in the Mesopotamian economy, I.J. Gelb, 'Household and Family in Ancient Mesopotamia', in E. Lipinski (ed.), *State and Temple Economy in the Ancient Near East* (Louvain, 1979), pp. 1-98.

Chapter 4. *Politics and Culture of the Early State*

Origins of writing, D. Schmandt-Besserat, *Before Writing* (2 vols.; Austin, 1992). The Susa sequence, A. Le Brun and F. Vallat, 'L'origine de l'écriture à Suse', *Cahiers de la Délégation Archéologique Française en Iran* 8 (1978), pp. 11-59. On the archaic texts from Uruk, see the special issues of the journals *Visible Language* 15/4 (1981) and *World Archaeology* 17/3 (1986). Sealings, P. Ferioli and E. Fiandra, 'Clay-sealings from Arslantepe VI A: Administration and Bureaucracy', *Origini* 12 (1983), pp. 455-509; *Archives before Writing* (Rome, 1994).

2. *The Sexagesimal World*

Lexical Lists, H.J. Nissen, 'Bemerkungen zur Listenliteratur Vorderasiens im 3. Jahrtausend', in L. Cagni (ed.), *La lingua di Ebla* (Naples, 1981), pp. 99-108. Administrative standardization, cf. R.K. Englund, 'Administrative Timekeeping in Ancient Mesopotamia', *Journal of the Economic and Social History of the Orient* 31 (1988), pp. 121-85.

3. *The House of God*

The concept of the temple-city goes back to A. Deimel, *Sumerische Tempelwirtschaft zur Zeit Urukaginas und seiner Vorgänger* (Rome, 1931), and A. Schneider, *Die sumerische Tempelstadt* (Essen, 1920). For the correction of the view, see I.M. Diakonoff, 'The Structure of Near Eastern Society before the Middle of the 2nd Millennium B.C.', *Oikumene* 3 (1982), pp. 7-100. Rejection of the centrality of the temple, I.J. Gelb, 'On the Alleged Temple and State Economies in Ancient Mesopotamia', in *Studi in onore di E. Volterra*, VI (Milan, 1969), pp. 137-54; B.R. Foster, 'A New Look at the Sumerian Temple State', *Journal of the Economic and Social History of the Orient* 24 (1981), pp. 225-41. Rejection of the temple character of the Eanna buildings, J.D. Forrest, 'La grande architecture obeidienne: sa forme et sa fonction', in *Préhistoire de la Mésopotamie* (Paris, 1987), pp. 385-423.

4. *Ideological Mobilization*
Collection of proverbs, B. Alster, *The Instructions of Šuruppak* (Copenhagen, 1974). On debate poems, J.J. van Dijk, *La sagesse suméro-accadienne* (Leiden, 1953); B. Alster and H. Vanstiphout, 'Lahar and Ashnan', *Acta Sumerologica* 9 (1987), pp. 1-43. The Sumerian myths are translated in J. Bottéro and S.N. Kramer, *Lorsque les dieux faisaient l'homme* (Paris, 1989).

Chapter 5. *Center and Periphery*

1. *The Regional System*
On the 'world system' (derived from I. Wallerstein, *The Modern World System* [New York, 1974]) in early Near Eastern history, P. Kohl, 'The Use and Abuse of World System Theory: The Case of the Pristine West Asian State', *Advances in Archaeological Method and Theory* 11 (1987), pp. 1-35. For Uruk, G. Algaze, *The Uruk World System* (Chicago, 1993). On the complexity in the Near Eastern environment, lastly, K. Butzer, 'Environmental Change in the Near East and Human Impact on the Land', in J. Sasson (ed.), *Civilizations of the Ancient Near East* (New York 1995), I, pp. 123-52. For a historical approach two contributions by R. McC. Adams still remain fundamental, in *City Invincible* (Chicago, 1960), pp. 23-34 and 275-81, and 'Strategies of Maximization, Stability, and Resilience in Mesopotamian Society, Settlement, and Agriculture', *Proceedings of the American Philosophical Society* 122 (1978), pp. 329-35.

2. *Primary and Secondary State Formation*
On the concept of secondary state formation, B. Price, 'Secondary State Formation: An Explanatory Model', in R. Cohen and E. Service (eds.), *The Origin of the State* (Philadelphia, 1978), pp. 161-86. A comparison of two cases of primary state formation (Mesopotamia and Mesoamerica), R. McC. Adams, *The Evolution of Urban Society* (Chicago, 1966). On the main peripheral sites, E. Strommenger, *Habuba Kabira* (Mainz, 1980); M.R. Behm-Blancke, *Hassek Höyök* (Tübingen, 1992); D. Canal, 'La terrasse haute de l'acropole de Suse', *Cahiers de la Délégation Archéologique Française en Iran* 9 (1978), pp. 11-55. On the case of Arslantepe, M. Frangipane, 'Local Components in the Development of Centralized Societies in Syro-Anatolian Regions', in *Archaeologia anatolica et mesopotamica A. Palmieri dedicata* (Rome, 1993), pp. 133-61.

3. *The Problem of Collapse*
On the question of collapse, N. Yoffee and G.L. Cowgill (eds.), *The Collapse of Ancient States and Civilizations* (Tuscon, 1988); J.A. Tainter, *The Collapse of Complex Societies* (Cambridge, 1988). Regionalization in the post-Uruk period, A. Palmieri, 'Eastern Anatolia and Early Mesopotamian Urbanization: Remarks on Changing Relations', in *Studi in onore di S. Puglisi* (Rome, 1985), pp. 191-213; U. Finkbeiner and W. Röllig (eds.), *Ğamdat Nasr. Period or Regional Style?* (Wiesbaden, 1986).

Date BCE	Archaeological period	Syria	Upper Mesopotamia	Lower Mesopotamia	Iran
6000	Neolithic		Halaf (5000–4500)		
4500	Chalcolithic			Early Ubaid (4500–4000)	
				Late Ubaid (4000–3500)	
3500	'Urban Revolution'			Early Uruk (3500–3200)	Proto-Elanite (3100–2700)
				Late Uruk (3200–3000)	
3000	Early Bronze		Ninevite 5 (3000–2350)	Early Dynastic I (2900–2750)	
				Early Dynastic II (2750–2600)	
				Early Dynastic IIIa (2600–2500)	
2500		Ebla (2500–2300)		Early Dynastic IIIb (2500–2350)	
				Akkad (2350–2200)	
				Neo-Summerian (2100–2000)	
2000	Middle Bronze		Old Assyrian (1950–1750)	Old Babylonian (2000–1600)	
1500					

Figure 1. *Chronology of the prehistoric and proto-historic cultures of Mesopotamia.*

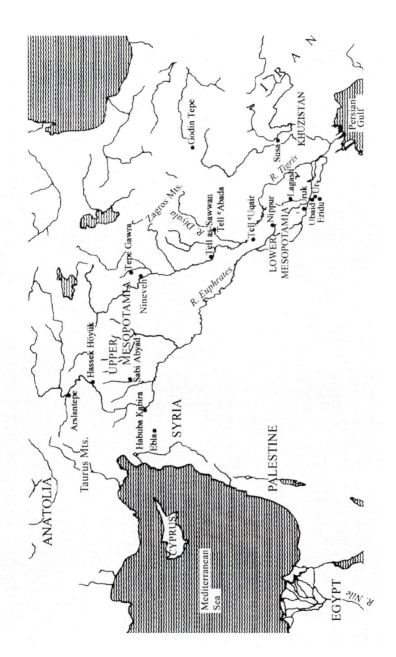

Figure 2. *Mesopotamia in the Uruk Period.*

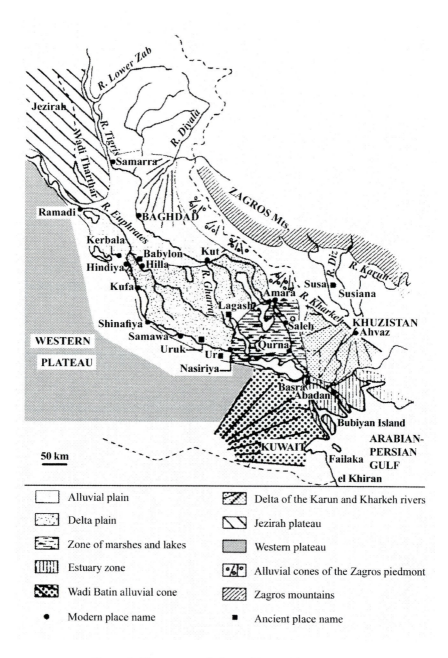

Figure 3. *The geo-morphology of Lower Mesopotamia.*

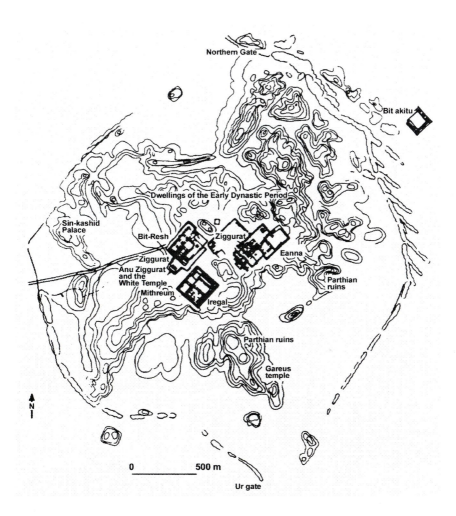

Figure 4. *Uruk: General plan.*

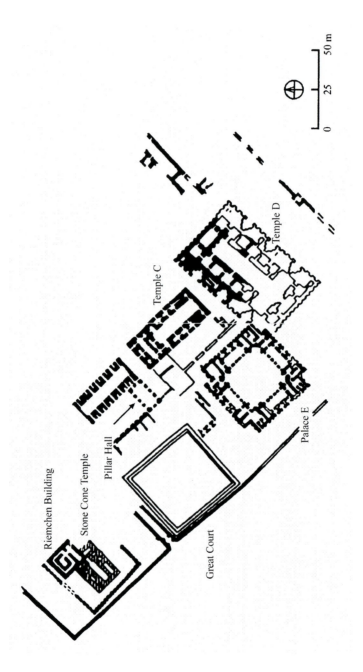

Figure 5. *Uruk: The Eanna sacred precinct.*

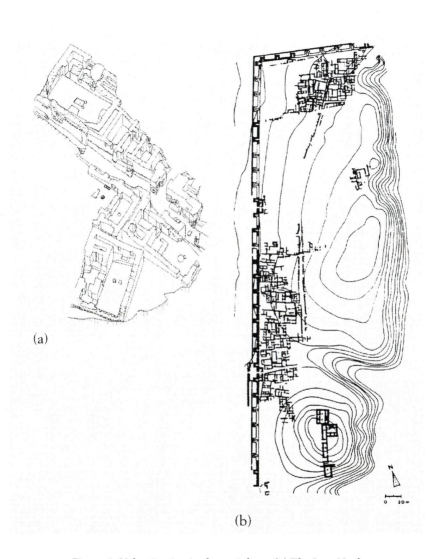

(a)

(b)

Figure 6. *Urbanization in the periphery: (a) The Late Uruk complex of Arslantepe; (b) Habuba Kabira: General plan.*

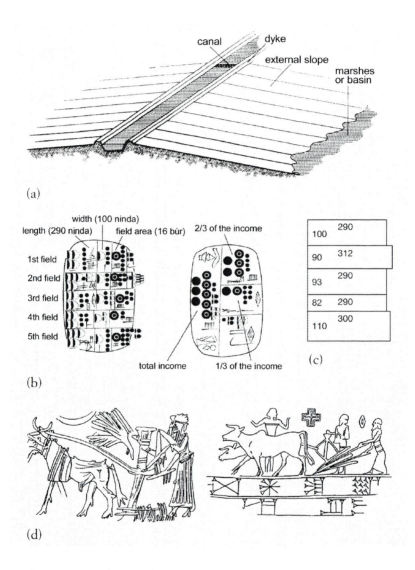

Figure 7. *Agriculture in the Late Uruk period: (a) scheme of the 'long field';
(b-c) cadastral tablet and its graphic reproduction; (d) the seeder-plow in
Mesopotamian glyptic.*

(a)

ANIMAL CLASSIFICATION

	SHEEP	GOATS	CATTLE
Adult female	U_8 ⊞	UD_5 ⊞	ÁB ◇
Adult male	UDUNITA ⊕◇	MÁŠ +◇	
Young female	KIR_{11} ▣▷	EŠGAR ⊟	AMAR-SAL ⟫▷
Young male	SILANITA ▣◇	MAŠ +	AMAR-KUR ⟫
Produce	◁	▭▷	▯▷

(b)

W 17729GI

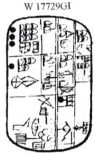

(c)

total of sheep	39
dead sheep	2
SU and other deductions	15
one-year old sheep	0
(remaining adult sheep)	22
new-born lambs	11

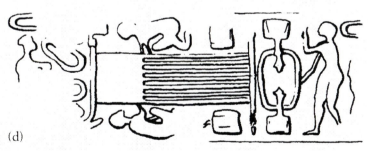

(d)

Figure 8. *Agro-pastoral activity in the Late Uruk period: (a) Threshing sledge on a seal from Arslantepe; (b) animal terminology in the Uruk texts; (c) tablet with the description of a herd; (d) weaving scene on a seal from Susa.*

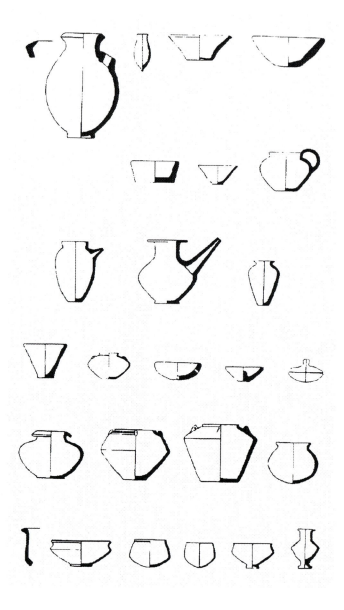

Figure 9. *Pottery of the Late Uruk period.*

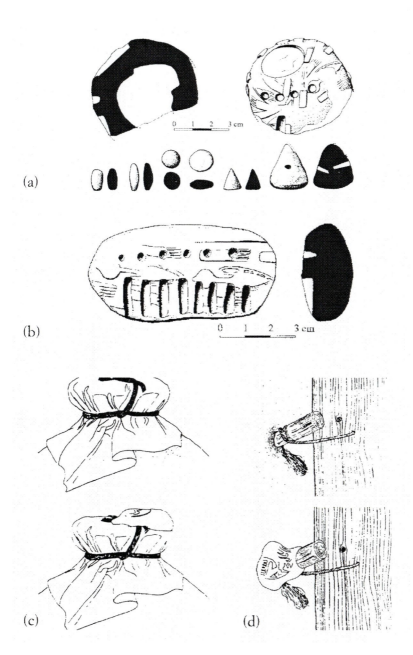

Figure 10. *Recording and guarantees: (a) Bulla and tokens;*
(b) numerical tablet; (c) jar sealing; (d) door sealing.

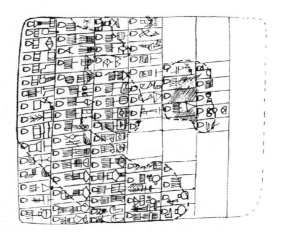

(a)

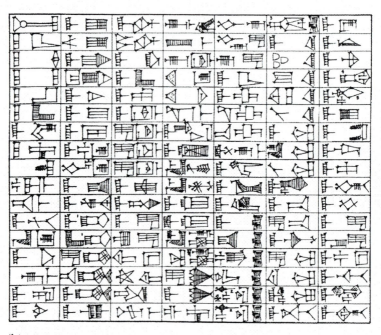

(b)

Figure 11. *Lexical list of professional names:*
(a) Tablet of the Uruk III period; (b) Tablet of the Early Dynastic period.

Adams, Robert McCormick: ix, 70
administered trade: 8, 36, 41, 46
administration: 2, 8, 12-13, 20, 25, 28, 30, 32-59, 72-76
Afghanistan: 49
Akkad: 27, 29, 75
Akkadian language: 27-28
Anatolia: 39, 43, 49, 67-68, 72-74
animals: 34, 37, 39, 43, 53, 63, 68
animal traction: 15-19
archaic texts: viii, 12-14, 16-17, 37, 53
archive: 41, 55-56, 60
army: 50-51
Arslantepe: 39, 63, 70-74
assembly: 61, 63
Atramhasis: 65

barley: 8, 24, 32-38, 44, 56, 58-59, 69
barter: 45, 47, 61
Boserup, Ester: 11
bowl: 47-48
bulla: 53-54
Burckhardt, Jacob: 5
burial: 22, 30
butter: 37

canal: 6, 16, 18-19, 24, 27, 45, 51, 59, 64-65
capital: 6-8
Central Asia: 68, 71
Chalcolithic: 39, 54, 67, 73
cheese: 37
chiefdom: ix, 9-10, 12, 20-21, 24, 26, 30, 33-34, 54, 69, 74
Childe, V. Gordon: vii, 2, 5-7, 9-12, 15, 19, 44-45
city: 10, 15, 25, 27, 43-44, 47, 60-61, 64, 69, 71

clan: 21, 24, 26, 28
colony: 43, 67, 72-74
complex society: 1, 10, 36, 40, 44, 62
copper: 42-43, 48-49, 59, 75
corvée: 21, 24, 33-35, 45, 50-51, 65
crafts: 20, 40, 44-51
cuneiform: viii, 12, 17, 53
Cyprus: 49

date palm: 6, 35, 65, 69
debate poem: 64-65
defense: 21, 50-52, 64
Diakonoff, Igor: 60
Dilmun: 43

Eanna: 2, 12, 24, 30, 53, 61, 63, 73-74, 80, 88
Early Dynastic period: 13, 27, 29, 53, 60-61, 74
Early Uruk period: 15, 18, 22, 24-25, 54, 73
Ebla: 46, 74-75
Egypt: 1, 29, 39, 70, 72
elite: 19-20, 22, 25-26, 28, 30, 52, 54, 60, 64, 70, 75-76
emmer: 32
Engels, Friedrich: 5
Eridu: 23, 27
exchange: viii-ix, 25, 36, 39, 42, 44-45, 48, 50, 52, 54, 56, 60-64, 69-72
extended family: 27, 29, 31, 34, 60

family: 6-7, 16, 19-21, 24-35, 39, 44-50, 54-56, 60-61, 64
farmer: 6, 33, 64
Fiandra, Enrica: 55
Frangipane, Marcella: 71
Frank, Gunder: 68

Fried, Morton: 9
fuel: 34, 47, 49

goat: 36, 39, 69
Godin Tepe: 72-73
gold: 36, 47, 49
great organizations: 8, 25-26, 46, 59
Guti: 65

Habuba Kabira: 72-73
Halaf period: 54
Hassek Höyük: 73
Heichelheim, Fritz: 7-8
Herodotus: 17
hoe: 17, 19, 65
house: 22-24, 28, 46, 50, 64-65, 75

Indus Valley: 40, 43, 68, 70, 72
industrial revolution: vii, 3, 6, 8, 24
Iran: 43-44, 68, 72-73
irrigation: 7, 15-17, 24, 27-30, 32-33, 36,
    59-60, 68, 70, 75

Jacobsen, Thorkild: 63

Kula, Witold: 33

Lagash: 27
Lagash King List: 65
lapis lazuli: 44
late Uruk period: 2, 13, 15, 18, 25, 27, 30,
    34, 39, 42-43, 51, 72-74
lexical text: 13, 53, 55, 57
linen: 39
loans: 7, 43
long field: ix, 15-18, 20, 24, 27, 30, 33, 68,
    70
loom: 38-39, 46

magazine: 51, 55
market: 8, 41, 44, 48, 61, 70
Martu: 65
Marx, Karl: 5-7, 12, 24
merchant: 40-43, 50, 56
milk: 37, 57
milling: 38, 45-46
mode of production: 6-7
Morgan, Lewis Henry: 5
mould: 48-49
myth: 36, 44, 64-65

Neolithic: 1-3, 5, 10, 18, 23, 28, 44, 48,
    54, 56, 63
Neo-Sumerian period: 13, 27, 32, 34, 37,
    42, 48
Nile valley: 18, 39
Ninurta: 65
Nippur: 27
nuclear family: 27, 29-30

obsidian: 40
oikos: 28, 60
oil: 8, 39, 42, 47, 58-59
Oman: 43, 49
Oppenheim, A. Leo: 8
origins of cities: vii, ix, 5, 8
origins of writing: viii, 1-2, 53, 80

palace: 8, 25, 34, 36, 41, 46, 49-50, 60, 62,
    74-76
periphery: vii-viii, 21, 23, 27, 29-30, 35,
    39, 44, 49, 63, 65, 67-76
Polanyi, Karl: 8, 41
potter: 47, 57
potter's wheel: 22, 47-48
pottery: 22, 26, 44, 47, 74
primitive democracy: 63
Proto-Elamite: 74
proverb: 64

rain: 27, 32, 37, 67, 76
ration: 8, 30, 33-36, 38, 46, 48, 50-51, 56-
    58
redistribution: 8, 13, 25, 32-36, 41, 45,
    48-49, 52, 54, 61-62, 64, 70, 74
religion: vii, 6, 25, 63-64, 75-76

Sabi Abyad: 54
scribe: 53-58
seal: 46, 53-55
seeder-plow: 16-19, 33, 65
semi-precious stone: 22, 35-36, 40, 49, 59
Service, Elman: 9
sexagesimal system: 57-59
shearing: 36, 38, 40, 45
sheep: 32, 36-40, 45, 53, 57, 69
shepherd: 37, 42, 56, 74
sickle: 17-18
silver: 43, 49, 59, 65
slave: 38, 45, 60
staple finance: 8, 35

storage house: 18, 48, 50, 54-57, 60, 62
Sumer: 6
Sumerian language: 28, 32-33, 44
surplus: 6-8, 15, 19-26, 33-36, 38, 42, 44-45, 62, 74, 76
Susa: 23, 53-54, 73-74
Susiana: 67, 73-74

tablet: viii, 53, 55-56
Taurus mountains: 68
Tell Abada: 22, 30
Tell es-Sawwan: 22
Tell 'Uqair: 23
temple: 2, 6-8, 13, 16, 22-27, 30, 33-39, 41, 45-46, 49-53, 56, 59-64, 73-76
temple-city: 60-61
Tepe Gawra: 23
textile: 8, 36, 38-39, 42-45, 58
thresher sledge: 17-18
tin: 48-49
token: viii, 30, 53-55
trade: 8, 11, 36, 39-44, 46, 49, 56, 68, 76
Transcaucasia: 74
tribe: 9, 28

Ubaid period: 18, 22, 24-25, 28, 30, 32, 35, 39, 43, 48, 54, 67, 70

Umma: 27
Ur: 27, 53, 61
urban revolution: 3, 5-7, 9, 12-13, 15, 19, 24-25, 28-31, 38-39, 45, 49, 54, 62, 73
urbanization: 8, 15, 18, 25, 27-30, 33, 35-37, 50, 67-68, 72-76

village: 10, 16, 21, 23, 25-29, 33-34, 44, 47-48, 51, 60-61, 64, 74

Wallerstein, Immanuel: 67-68
war: 11, 38, 50-51
weaving: 36, 38, 45-46, 49-50
wheat: 32-33, 64
Wittfogel, Karl: 15
Wolf, Eric: 68
wood: 36, 40, 43, 46, 49, 68
wool: 8, 36-40, 56-59
world system: viii, 67-68
writing: vii-ix, 1-2, 12, 18, 53-57, 59, 63, 74

Yoffee, Norman: 9

Zagros mountains: 37, 68

Printed in the United States
56338LVS00001BB

9 781845 531911